YUM

YOUR ULTIMATE MANUAL
FOR GOOD NUTRITION

DAINA KALNINS, MSC, RD

Lobster Press ™

Published by Lobster Press™
1620 Sherbrooke Street West, Suites C & D
Montréal, Québec H3H 1C9
Tel. (514) 904-1100 • Fax (514) 904-1101 • www.lobsterpress.com

Publisher: Alison Fripp
Editors: Meghan Nolan, Lindsay Cornish
Contributing Writers: Lindsay Cornish and Shiran Teitelbaum
Editorial Assistant: Shiran Teitelbaum
Graphic Design: *the*BookDesigners
Production Manager: Tammy Desnoyers
Spot illustrations of fruits and food characters: iStock/Simon Oxley

Readers should discuss any significant changes in their current diet or activity level
with their parents and physician before they actually make the changes. The publisher
and the author encourage parents to exercise caution and good judgment when
engaging in any activity with their children, and neither Lobster Press nor the author
can be held responsible for any accidents or illnesses that may occur and will not be
responsible for sickness attributable to food allergies or sensitivities.

The personal essays in this book were submitted as original work, and in some cases,
were edited for clarity. The statements, opinions, views, and comments reflect the
views of the independent contributors and not those of Lobster Press.

Library and Archives Canada Cataloguing in Publication

Kalnins, Daina   YUM: your ultimate manual for good nutrition / Daina Kalnins ;
illustrator: Paula Becker.

Includes bibliographical references and index. ISBN 978-1-897073-72-8
1. Nutrition–Juvenile literature. I. Becker, Paula, 1958- II. Title.

RA784.K29 2008   j613.2   C2007-905474-9

David Hadgrave
"Mainse

GRANDSON DAVID

DEDICATED TO MY DEAR CHILDREN, NATALI AND MATIS
-DAINA KALNINS GRANPA DAVE
GET WELL SOON.

CONTENTS

FOREWORD
BY PAUL FINKELSTEIN

Food is a tricky thing.

We all need it to survive, as food is the fuel for life. But it shouldn't become just a necessity. It should remain exciting and stimulating to the taste buds – a learning experience with each and every mouthful. However, taste is only one part of the eating equation. As the yummy morsels are digested, every part of your body shares in the experience. This can be a pretty scary thought when you consider what we put into our bellies some days!

As a teacher, I try to get my students to understand where food comes from and to learn about preparing it, tasting it, eating it, and digesting it. At the Screaming Avocado Café, the funky school eatery run by my students, I teach the idea of "seed to table and beyond" – we explore food from where it grows right through to when it enters your mouth and what it does for your body.

You too can start learning about and appreciating your eating experience right now. Preparing a meal with fresh ingredients is the first step. Asking your parents if you can help out in planning the menu and cooking it could be a great growing experience for everyone. After this, sitting at the dinner table and eating with your family and sharing stories about the day can broaden the food experience even more. This might also happen at school during lunch break. Try new tastes – even if cooked fish with the head attached freaks you out (I have to admit the eyeballs are kinda scary). It may look freaky, but give it a try! Even if you didn't like Brussels sprouts when your Aunt Wendy made them for you, try making them yourself with some secret ingredients you enjoy! Maybe you'll find something new that you like.

As parents of three young children, my wife Amanda and I are constantly challenged to find foods that our children will enjoy. As chefs we strive to feed them freshly prepared meals from healthy ingredients. For the most part, they enjoy the food we prepare, especially roast chicken with a vegetable stir-fry and rice. Of course, there are occasions when they think we're crazy – chicken livers, pickled herring, pig tails, and fish-head soup just don't seem to agree with their taste buds. However, we also allow our kids to be kids – they occasionally get junk foods like ice cream, chocolate bars, and chips. They also eat out in fast food restaurants as a special treat every so often. We think that by creating a sane logic around food that is based on balance (balance of different foods, balance of healthy foods and not-so-healthy foods, balance of food and exercise), our kids are developing a good understanding of how to eat for life.

Hey, I even have my own "guilty pleasure" foods that I dive into now and then: French fries, pizza, and pretty much anything chocolate (even chocolate-covered grasshoppers when I can get them). But I also love fresh fruits, vegetables, and fish ... everything in balance.

I have learned that it is really important to understand how your body works and what it needs to work at its best. This is where YUM: Your Ultimate Manual for Good Nutrition comes in. This book will give you the information needed to understand how your body works, what nutrients you need to keep on going, and what foods are best for you. The recipes will provide you with some tasty ideas and will give you the opportunity to teach your family a thing or two about cooking and about the eating experience. Most importantly, you'll learn that eating can be an amazing lifetime adventure full of surprises and pleasure. Enjoy the journey!

© 2008 Paul Finkelstein

ACKNOWLEDGMENTS

What a great opportunity to be able to share nutrition knowledge with kids, through the writing of this book. I am so grateful to all at Lobster Press, especially to Alison Fripp and Meghan Nolan for their support on this. A huge thanks to Meghan and to Lindsay Cornish for helping to organize the material so that the messages about healthy eating are clear and concise – and for putting the fun into this book. I am thrilled to have the very talented Paula Becker add the illustrations to the words. Thank you, Paula.

My thanks to all of my colleagues at Sick Kids. I have learned and continue to learn so much from all of you. A special thanks to Debbie O'Connor – your support means so much.

To my dear friends, thanks for listening and for kind words and thoughts: Terri and Jeff, Alexa and Jake, Maureen, Gloria, Wendy, Joann, Joanne N., Joanne S., Charlotte M., and Jennifer B., Nicole, Randi, Monica, Erica, Vivian, Jennifer, and Morry.

And finally, with a BIG hug, I thank Natali, Matis, and Blair for making life so sweet and wonderful. I am so proud of you both, Natali and Matt, and love you with all my heart and more. Blair, you support me always, and I am so lucky to have you. Milu jus!

AUTHOR'S NOTE

As you read this book, you will probably want to make some changes and try some new things in order to make good nutrition and exercise a part of your life. That's awesome! But it is really important that you talk to your parents and your doctor before you make any changes to your diet or to your level of exercise. And a note to parents: neither Lobster Press nor the author can be held responsible for illness, including food allergies, or injuries that may result if you or your child tries anything listed in this book.

INTRODUCTION

You've probably heard, "Eat that, it's good for you!" or "Don't eat that, it's so bad for you!" over and over again. But have you ever wondered why certain foods are good for you, while others are not?

Maybe you're really into the idea of eating healthy, but you're left wondering, "What does my body actually need to be healthy?"

Or maybe you already make a habit of healthy eating, but you're asking yourself, "How can I make healthy eating delicious, and even (gasp)... fun?"

As a dietitian, I have spent a lot of time looking at how kids eat and the food choices they make. And many people, adults and kids alike, just don't really know enough about why eating well is so important. YUM shows you the clear reasons why certain foods are better for you than others. It shows you what your body needs to be healthy and how to make good food choices. Most importantly, this book is about being real – we don't want you to become nutritional robots! You can choose to have your slice of chocolate cake and eat it too, as long as you balance it out with healthy, nutrient-rich food choices.

YUM is packed with all the info and tips you need to feel empowered to make healthy choices. You'll start by taking a close look at food labels and the parts of food that your body really needs. In Chapter 1, you'll find out about *macronutrients* and learn how they give you energy to fuel your body. Chapter 2 shows you the smaller – but very necessary – parts of your food, the *micronutrients*. You'll then follow a cheese sandwich through your digestive tract in Chapter 3, and you'll see how your body breaks food down to absorb nutrients. You'll also see how exercise and nutrition are both vital to keeping your body balanced. Chapter 4 has tons of YUMmy recipes, meals, and snack ideas that you can use. Then, Chapter 5 shows you how to make healthy choices no matter where you are – at home, in school, at the grocery store, or in a restaurant.

Along the way, you'll come across snappy sidebars, such as:

1. "Did You Know?" "Food Facts," and "Fast Bites," which give you extra tidbits about food and health.
2. "Good Ideas," which offer things you can do right now to get on the road to good nutrition.
3. "Q&As," which answer some of the most common nutrition questions.

4. "How Real Kids Eat Right" tips, which give kids like you a chance to have a say about what and how they eat.
5. "Celebs Say" sections, which show how some of today's celebrities make healthy eating a part of their lives.

YUM even has a section called "Healthy Eating & Exercise Tools," a glossary, and a list of online resources that give you even more information about healthy eating. And after you've read through the book, take the "pledge" on page 171 and then challenge yourself (and your family!) to participate in the "six-month challenge" on page 172.

Ready to get your taste of healthy eating and see why it's so important? Your new knowledge will be something you can use for the rest of your life.

SO LET'S DIG IN AND GET STARTED!

CHAPTER

1

What's in our Food Anyway?
Part I

Food is everywhere. It's on TV, online, in magazines, on billboards – it's even in your house! You just can't avoid it, and you certainly can't live without it. Deciding what to eat every day among the many, many choices you have can be really tough: What do I really want to eat right now? What do I need to eat to keep me growing and healthy? What foods will satisfy my hunger, my taste buds, and keep me strong?

In the following pages, you are going to see that you can have it all: tasty, filling food that helps your body move and grow. (Psst! It's all about variety!)

First, you'll need to get up close and personal with nutrients, which are the parts of your food that your body needs every day.

READY? LET'S GO FOR IT.

CHECK THE LABEL

If you want to know what's in your food, the best place to start is the nutrition panel on a food label. This panel gives you all the information you need to know about your food.

In the "Nutrition Facts" on a food label, you can find the following information:

⊕ Serving size: How much of that food you should eat in one sitting.

⊕ Calories in one serving: How much energy your body will get from one serving of that food.

⊕ Macronutrient content in one serving: How much fat, carbohydrate, and protein your body will get from one serving of that food (these measurements are given in grams and in the percentage (%) of your Daily Value).

⊕ Micronutrient content in one serving: How much sodium and certain vitamins and minerals you will get from one serving (this is given in % of your Daily Value). (Of course, not all foods, like fresh fruits, vegetables, or meats, have a label. To find out the nutrition info of these foods, check out the resource pages at the back of the book).

Nutrition Facts

Serving Size 1 cup (228g)
Servings Per Container 2

Amount Per Serving

Calories 250	Calories from Fat 110

	% Daily Value*
Total Fat 12g	18%
Saturated Fat 3g	15%
Trans Fat 1.5g	
Cholesterol 30mg	10%
Sodium 470mg	20%
Total Carbohydrate 31g	10%
Dietary Fiber 0g	0%
Sugars 5g	
Protein 5g	

Vitamin A	4%
Vitamin C	2%
Calcium	20%
Iron	4%

* Percent Daily Values are based on a 2,000 calorie diet.
  Your Daily Values may be higher or lower depending on
  your calorie needs:

	Calories:	2,000	2,500
Total Fat	Less than	66g	80g
Sat Fat	Less than	20g	25g
Cholesterol	Less than	300mg	300mg
Sodium	Less than	2,400mg	2,400mg
Total Carbohydrate		300g	375g
Dietary Fiber		25g	30g

Source: U.S. Food and Drug Administration (FDA)

NOTE: This food label is from North America – in other parts of the world, food labels might look different, and / or give other information.

A food's packaging will also give you the list of ingredients in that food. The ingredients are what gives your food its nutrients. A list of ingredients shows everything that was mixed together to make those crackers, or cookies, or jam, but without showing you exactly how much of each ingredient was used (because that would give away their secret recipes!).

Q: WHAT IS A SERVING?

A: A serving is the amount of a particular food that a person should eat at one meal or snack. Food manufacturers decide how much food is in a serving of their product, and they include that measurement on the food's label. A serving can be measured in many different ways, depending on the kind of food: sometimes, the measurement is one "piece" of that thing, like a slice of bread. For other foods, a serving is measured in ounces (grams), or cups (milliliters).

The problem is that often, our idea of a serving is VERY different from what the manufacturer had in mind.

GOOD IDEA!

Find out how your serving size compares to the one on the label: Take out your favorite box of cereal. Pour your regular amount of cereal into a bowl (but don't pour any milk on top – you won't get the right measurement!). Take out some measuring cups and measure how much cereal is in the bowl. Write down the number on a piece of paper. Then, find the serving size on the nutrition label and write that number on your piece of paper. Now compare the two numbers: are you eating more or less than the serving size? Does that mean you are eating more or less nutrients than are listed on the label?

The bottom line about servings: If you decide to eat more or less than the serving on the label, that is your choice to make. But, you need to know that you will be getting more or less nutrients than the label indicates. While that's okay sometimes, if it happens consistently with a lot of the foods you eat, your body might get out of balance (you'll find out more about how that happens on pages 105-108).

Q: WHAT DOES "% DAILY VALUE" MEAN?

A: There is a certain amount of each nutrient that you need to take in every day so that you stay healthy. For example, when you get all of your carbohydrate, you are getting 100% of what you need for that day. It is just like if you get all the answers right on a test, you score 100%.

When you look at the nutrition facts on a food label, you can see that each nutrient has a percentage next to it. This tells you that in one serving of that food, you will get that percentage of that nutrient for that day. It's simple: if a label shows that one serving of cereal will give you 20% of your DV of fiber, that means you're getting 20% of the fiber that you need for that day. So do you have all the fiber you need for that day? Nope, you'll have to get some more from other foods, because 20% is less than 100%.

Keep in mind that the % Daily Values that are given are technically for adults (I guess the food manufacturers didn't realize that kids could know so much about nutrition!). While adults need different amounts of nutrients than you do, the % Daily Values are still a great way to see if you are getting what you need from a serving of that food.

How can you tell if a food is a "good source" of a nutrient? If it says that a serving gives you 15% of your DV or more, then you can consider it a good source of that nutrient.[1, 2]

Q: IS THERE AN A+ FOOD THAT WILL GIVE ME 100% OF MY DAILY VALUE FOR ALL OF MY NUTRIENTS?

A: Nope, there's no such thing as one "perfect food" that gives you everything you need for a day. While a certain food might be a fantastic source of some nutrients, it might not be such a great source of other nutrients. For example, a serving of spinach is packed with fiber, vitamin A, vitamin C, calcium, and iron, but it only contains a little protein. Or take a serving of lean chicken: it is loaded with protein, niacin, and phosphorus, but it contains no carbohydrate whatsoever.

So, try to include lots of different foods in your meals and snacks. That way, your body will be more likely to get everything it needs.

Q: Why are the Ingredients in that Order?

A: While the manufacturers do not reveal how much of each ingredient is used to create their foods, they give you a hint about which ingredients they used in large quantities, and which were used in small quantities. In the list, the first ingredient is the one that was used in the biggest amount. For example, on a box of cereal, the first ingredient might be whole grain oats. This means that the manufacturer used more whole grain oats than any other ingredient. The ingredient that is listed last is the one used in the smallest amount. Sometimes, the last ingredients can have really long names that are tough to read – these are chemicals called additives and you'll learn more about them on page 78.

Plain Yogurt

INGREDIENTS: CULTURED PASTEURIZED GRADE A NONFAT MILK, WHEY PROTEIN CONCENTRATE, PECTIN, CARRAGEENAN

Fruit Yogurt

INGREDIENTS: CULTURED GRADE A REDUCED FAT MILK, APPLES, HIGH FRUCTOSE CORN SYRUP, CINNAMON, NUTMEG, NATURAL FLAVORS, AND PECTIN. CONTAINS ACTIVE YOGURT AND L. ACIDOPHILUS CULTURES.

Source: U.S. Food and Drug Administration (FDA)

Above are the ingredient lists for two yogurts. Yogurt is made mostly of milk, so that is why milk is the first ingredient in the list for both.

BREAKING IT DOWN

When we talk about what's in our food, we could look at the list of ingredients – after all, this list does tell us exactly what things were mixed together to make our food. We can read the list of ingredients and say, "This granola is made of peanuts, raisins, sunflower seeds, and cashews. Awesome!" However, if you want to know if a particular food is nutritious, it makes a lot more sense to look at the parts of your food that your body really needs to grow and stay healthy, even though you can't really "see" these parts.

There are two kinds of nutrients that your body requires: macronutrients, which are large food parts ("macro" actually means "large") and micronutrients, which are small food parts (did you already guess that "micro" means "small"?). For now, let's focus on macronutrients (you'll learn all about micros in Chapter 2).

Macronutrients are the group of nutrients made of carbohydrates, fats, and proteins. Whether we're talking about a fruit, a candy bar, a burrito, or a peanut butter and jelly sandwich, every food contains at least one of these macronutrients. Your body needs a relatively large amount of these nutrients every day (so large that you can measure these amounts in grams). Your body needs carbohydrate and fat for energy, and protein for energy (sometimes) and to keep your muscles moving.

First, let's take a look at how energy flows into your body through what you eat, and how energy flows out of your body when you do activities.

Whether you're walking, sitting, running, or even reading this book, everything you do requires energy. Even sleeping requires energy! Think about it: while you're asleep, your heart is still pumping, your lungs are still filling up with air and letting that air out, and most importantly, your brain is still controlling everything that is happening throughout your body.

The carbohydrate, fat, and protein that you eat all contain energy that your body needs. This energy is measured in a unit called calories. So, if we say that a serving of food contains 50 calories, that means that the food will provide you with 50 units of energy.

Q: DO THE 3 MACRONUTRIENTS EACH GIVE ME THE SAME AMOUNT OF ENERGY?

A. Actually, carbs, fats, and proteins each give you a different amount of calories to fuel your body. Let's say we take one gram of each macro and compare: one gram of carbohydrate gives your body four calories of energy; one gram of fat fuels you with nine calories of energy; and one gram of protein gives your body four calories of energy. So, not all macros are created equal – fat is a heavy hitter!

Did You Know?

ENERGY IN: The nutritional labels on foods will tell you exactly how many calories, or how much energy your body will get, from one serving. But have you ever wondered about stuff that doesn't have a label? Here is the approximate calorie content of some common foods:

- 1 cup water = 0
- 1 carrot = 25
- 1 apple = 95
- 1 chicken leg = 180
- 1 avocado = 220
- 1 hamburger with everything on it = 295
- 1 medium order of French fries = 385

To find out the number of calories in other foods without labels, check out our resource pages at the back of the book.

Did You Know?

ENERGY OUT: The harder you play, the more you burn. When you're watching TV or surfing the Net, you're using way fewer calories than if you were skateboarding or playing tennis.

Here are the approximate calories used by a kid who weighs about 70 lb (32 kg) doing each activity for one hour:

Bicycling = 250
Tennis = 225
Soccer = 220
Bowling = 100
Walking = 80
Sleeping = 30
Watching TV = 15

At least an hour of activity or exercise keeps your body healthy and your muscles strong. So get moving!

So how much energy do you need each day? That depends on your age, weight, and your overall level of activity. Generally, kids between the ages of 8 and 13 need between 1600 and 2600 calories each day. Somewhere in that range is your healthy zone; this is where you strike a balance between the energy going into your body from your macronutrients and the energy that goes out your body when you exercise and go through your daily activities.

In Chapter 3, you will learn even more about how this balancing act works and how to deal if your body is out of balance.

All right, now that you know why macros are so important, let's take a look at each one of them and find out where you can get them.

HANG ON!
WHAT ABOUT THE FOOD GROUPS AND THE FOOD PYRAMID?

You've probably learned about fruits & vegetables, cereals & grains, meats & pulses, milk & dairy foods, and fats & oils in school by studying food guides or a food pyramid. Once you've learned about how to create healthy meals, we'll take a look at how to use the food groups to jazz them up.

If you haven't already learned about the food groups and the food pyramid, check out these sites:

→ US FDA "MyPyramid": http://www.mypyramid.gov/kids/index.html
→ Canada Food Guide: http://www.hc-sc.gc.ca/fn-an/food-guide-aliment/myguide-monguide/index_e.html

CALLING ON CARBS

Carbohydrates can be found in fruits, many vegetables, bread, cereal, grains, pastas, and milk. You can also get carbs from fruit juices, fruit drinks, sodas, and candy. While all of these foods contain carbs, some carbs are better for you than others. Read on.

Some carbohydrates are called "complex carbohydrates." They are called "complex" because they are made up of many smaller parts. This means it takes your body a long time to break down complex carbohydrates, and this gives you longer lasting energy.

One complex carb that people talk about a lot is fiber; it is a complex carb that your body cannot break down. Certain foods, like whole grain bread, fruits with the skin on, and raw veggies are good sources of this carb. It turns out that fiber plays an important role in your digestive system. For more info about that, turn to page 97.

FOOD FACT
WHOLE GRAINS FOR ME!

Grains like wheat, oats, rice, quinoa, millet, and spelt are really great sources of long-lasting complex carbohydrates, including fiber, and micronutrients. When these grains are used as ingredients in a processed food, sometimes the manufacturer will keep all of the healthy parts of the grain intact. Intact grains are called "whole grains" and you will see them in the list of ingredients: "whole wheat flour," "whole oat flour," and "brown rice flour" are examples of whole grains in action.

Other times, the manufacturer will remove the healthy part of the grain. These grains will be listed as "wheat flour," "oat flour," or "rice flour." Often, when manufacturers take away the healthy part, they will add in vitamins and minerals that will boost the nutrients in your food. This is called enriching, and you'll read more about that on page 77. While enriching foods can sometimes be a really good thing, doesn't it make more sense for you to eat foods that are naturally full of the complex carbs and micronutrients that your body needs?

So, as often as possible, choose a carb that is made with whole grain. Here are some ideas:

Instead of:
- white bread
- regular pasta
- white rice
- sweetened plain oatmeal, or flavored oatmeal

Choose:
- wholegrain bread
- whole wheat or whole grain pasta
- brown or mixed rice
- steel-cut oats

Other carbohydrates are called "simple sugars." There are many different simple sugars in different foods, including lactose, which is found in milk; sucrose, which can be found in maple syrup and molasses; and glucose and fructose, which can be found in fruits and honey. Simple sugars are... well, simple. They are not made up of many parts, which means it does not take long for them to be digested in your body.

Did You Know?

GETTING SCIENTIFIC!

The scientific name for carbs is "saccharides." Complex carbs are also known as polysaccharides ("poly" means "many"). Some simple sugars, like lactose and sucrose, are disaccharides ("di" means "two"), while others, like glucose and fructose, are monosaccharides ("mono" means "one").

Food Fact
THE MANY DISGUISES OF SUGAR

When you read the list of ingredients on a food label, be on the lookout for sugar in its many disguises (especially when it is near the beginning of the list): glucose, fructose, maltose, hydrolyzed starch, invert sugar, high-fructose corn syrup, and honey are all different kinds of sugar that are commonly added to sweet foods, like cakes, cookies, and jams. You can – and should – enjoy these foods from time to time (you'd be amazed at how often they pop up in birthday cakes and holiday desserts), but try to keep them to a minimum the rest of the time.

Good Idea!

Juice is a drink that comes in all kinds of flavors and mixtures. Some juices are mostly liquid from fruits (the label will read "100% juice"), while other drinks that are considered juices contain only a little bit of juice, and are mostly a mixture of water, sugars, and flavors (the labels often read "drink" or "cocktail"). Most juices, even the all-natural ones, contain a lot of sugar. This can be a problem if you are always reaching for juice when you're thirsty. In fact, you might be so used to drinking juice that you might not taste how sweet the juice really is anymore!

Try this: mix half juice and half water (or bubbly water) in a glass and drink that when you are thirsty. You'll still get the refreshing taste of the juice but with half of the sugar. Then, for even less sugar, try using more water and less juice next time.

29

When your body needs energy, it first taps into your carbohydrate supply. If you mostly fuel your body with complex carbs, you'll have long-lasting energy. If you mostly eat simple sugars, your energy level will spike quickly, then it will come crashing down quickly too. So if you're looking for a fuel to keep your body moving, complex carbs are definitely the way to go.

Did You Know?

Some people may be "lactose intolerant," which means that they cannot digest lactose, a simple sugar found in milk and milk products, because their bodies are lacking or do not have enough of the enzyme "lactase" to break down the lactose. If a person who is lactose intolerant eats or drinks a milk product, they will have a very upset stomach.

A lactose intolerance can be temporary and can happen after a person has had a bad stomach virus. When this happens, milk can slowly be brought back into the person's diet, which will give their body the chance to get used to digesting the lactose again.

For someone who has ongoing problems with poor lactose digestion, choosing products that have the milk sugar already digested (which can be found in grocery stores) is a good option.

Lactose intolerance is not a true allergy, like when someone has an allergy to peanuts. However, if you really do have a serious allergy to the protein in milk, then you should not drink or eat any milk or milk products at all.[3]

Did You Know?

Normally, when a person eats carbohydrates, their body produces special proteins (enzymes) to break those carbs down so that the cells can use them for energy (you will learn more about how your digestive system works in Chapter 3). Once the carbs are broken down, digested, and absorbed, a hormone called insulin makes sure that they can get into the cells.

People with diabetes either do not make enough insulin, or they make no insulin at all, which means their cells can't use the energy from carbs. Kids and some adults with diabetes need to get insulin into their bodies every day, either by injecting it with a needle, or by using an insulin pump.

Kids with diabetes need to balance their insulin intake with lots of exercise and a very healthy diet that includes complex carbohydrates in order to stay healthy.

Fantastic Fats!

The second macronutrient that our bodies need on a daily basis is fat. Fats are made up of smaller pieces called fatty acids. When we talk about fats, we usually talk about whether a fat is unsaturated or saturated.

Unsaturated fats can be divided into two groups: polyunsaturated and monounsaturated (remember that "poly" means "many," and "mono" means "one"). Polyunsaturated fats can be found in fish, like wild salmon and Atlantic mackerel, and whole grains. Monounsaturated fats can be found in nuts, oils, and avocados (YUM!). Typically, unsaturated fats are liquid at room temperature (think sunflower oil, corn oil, safflower oil, and canola oil), and they are much healthier for your body than saturated fats.

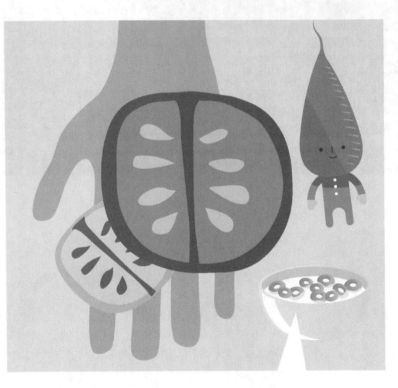

FOOD FACT

FISH JUICE?

Omega-3 fatty acids are a special kind of unsaturated fat that is really good for your body. Scientists have discovered that, despite the fact that we can get omega-3 from salmon, herring, trout, sardines, and some seeds and oils, we are just not getting enough. Because omega-3 serves many functions, such as controlling how well our bodies react to an infection, it is vital to make sure that our bodies get a good dose of this fatty acid.

So what are the food manufacturers doing about it? They are enriching all kinds of products with omega-3 fatty acids (some even from plant oils or from fish oil!). Foods that are currently fortified with omega-3 include juice, eggs, milk, and bread. While it's great that people have theses fortified foods to choose from, it also makes a lot of sense to get the omega-3 you need by eating foods like fish, seeds (flaxseeds are a great source of omega-3!), or nuts, like walnuts.

Saturated fats are found in many processed foods and fast foods, like hamburgers and hot dogs. While a little bit of saturated fat is okay for your body, it is common for both kids and adults to get way too much saturated fat.[4] If this happens over a long period of time, not only will your body get out of balance, but you can also have problems with your cholesterol levels and heart disease.[5]

It is a good idea for everyone to be aware of how much saturated fat they are eating. If you notice that even you (yes, you!) are getting a little too much of this persnickety fat, there are plenty of easy ways to cut back. Check it out:

→ If you eat steak, cut the fat away from the meat before you eat it.

→ If you eat burgers, choose ones that are made from lower-fat meat (the label may say "lean meat").

→ Bake cookies or cakes with a combination of butter (a saturated fat) and oil (a polyunsaturated fat), to help decrease the amount of saturated fat that is eaten.

→ Instead of drinking homogenized milk, switch to a lower fat milk, like 2% or 1% (or even skim milk if you're willing to make the leap!).

→ Use mashed avocado instead of butter on a sandwich.

→ Make your own salad dressings, using olive oil, canola oil, or sunflower oil, and different vinegars.

→ Try having one healthy vegetarian supper per week (you'll learn more about vegetarianism on pages 39 and 40).

FOOD FACT

Cholesterol is a substance that is frequently found in foods that contain lots of saturated fats, like meat, butter, and high-fat cheeses. The human body actually makes its own cholesterol too, and it can be found virtually everywhere in the body, like in the nervous system, the skin, and the muscles. However, some people have high levels of cholesterol in their blood. This happens not only in adults, but in kids who are overweight too.[6] So, to keep blood levels of cholesterol in check, try to keep those saturated fat foods to a minimum, and replace them with the healthier polyunsaturated ones. Exercise and having a healthy body weight also help.

Fat from food is a great energy source and also a great energy storage system in the body so that energy from fat can be used later (you will learn more about this in Chapter 3). However, fat does many other important jobs in your body too: it is vital in the production of hormones, which are the body's "messengers." Also, the body needs fat in order to absorb particular vitamins, such as A, D, E, and K, from the foods we eat. We will talk about this more in the next chapter.

Q: What are Trans Fats and Why aren't they Good for me?

A: During the late 1950s, the American Heart Association said that people should eat less saturated fats, because they found that people who ate more of these fats had more heart disease (but you already knew that from page 34!). So, the American Heart Association said that people should instead focus on getting healthier unsaturated fats from fish and vegetable oils.

In response, food manufacturers created an unsaturated fat that they could use just like a saturated fat in the foods they made. This fat was called trans fat, and everyone thought it was a great solution to the "fat problem" in America. However, scientists have since discovered that trans fats are also really bad for your health. In fact, many companies are now making foods without trans fats and they label their foods "trans fat free." (Remember, just because a food is labeled "trans fat free" doesn't mean that it is "fat free"). Check that label!

The issue of trans fat has become so huge that New York City banned trans fats in all of its restaurants' foods. This means that from the smallest hot dog cart to the biggest, fanciest restaurant in NYC, no one is allowed to put trans fats in their food. The Big Apple is really healthy!

THE POWER OF PROTEIN

The last of our macronutrients is protein. Proteins are made of a chain of small pieces called amino acids. There are 20 amino acids in all, and different combinations of these amino acids make different proteins. Your body makes over half of the amino acids that you need, so you have to get the rest from the food you eat.

So where can you get protein? You probably already know that protein is found in meats, chicken, fish, eggs, and milk products. But did you know that it can also be found in whole grains, legumes, nuts, and seeds?

The protein that is found in animal foods, like in meat and eggs, is full of all the amino acids that our bodies need. These are called "complete proteins." Other foods that have protein, like whole grains, nuts, and seeds, don't have all of the amino acids that our bodies need (except for quinoa). These are called "incomplete proteins." This means that a vegetarian, who is someone who only gets their protein from plant sources, must eat a wide variety of incomplete proteins to make sure they get all of the amino acids they need.

QUINOA: THE MOTHER GRAIN

Quinoa (pronounced keen-wah) is a grain that has been used for thousands of years. In fact, in some South American countries, it is known as the "Mother Grain." Quinoa is the only plant source of protein that is a complete protein.[7] So try to add quinoa to your meals by using it instead of rice in stir-fry dishes and casseroles.

WHAT YOU NEED TO KNOW ABOUT FOOD ALLERGIES

When a person has a food allergy, their body reacts to a protein in a particular food. There are many different foods that are likely to cause allergic reactions, including milk (see p. 30), fish, shellfish, wheat, eggs, and soy.

The most common food allergies these days are nut and peanut allergies. It is important that ALL kids know about nut and peanut allergies: when someone has this kind of allergy, their body reacts when they are exposed to the protein in nuts or peanuts. Some people's reactions are mild, while others' are very severe – a person's throat can swell and they can suffocate if they are not given medication in time. This is called anaphylaxis.

Everyone should know if their food contains nuts or traces of nuts (knowing how to read ingredient lists is so important!). If you have a nut, peanut, or any other kind of food allergy, be sure to carry your emergency medication with you at all times. If you don't have an allergy, be sure that you never bring foods that contain nuts or nut products to school or have them near friends or relatives who are allergic. And don't share your food with friends. While it seems like a nice thing to do, you don't want to accidentally share a food that will make them sick.

Food Fact
Don't blame the turkey!

Do you celebrate Thanksgiving or Christmas? If so, is turkey part of your family meal? Many people celebrate these holidays with lots of food, including a big turkey dinner, and some people have said that eating turkey makes them feel sleepy. Is it true – can the bird make you feel bushed? Scientists have found that turkey contains an amino acid called tryptophan, and tests have shown that it can make a person feel sleepy. However, this only happens if it is eaten in large quantities on an empty stomach. When you think about it, it is much more likely that people are sleepy during Christmas and Thanksgiving because they have eaten too much food, or maybe because they have not slept normally during of the holidays, or maybe because they feel so relaxed.[8] So don't blame the bird!

Fake Meats

Fake meats are foods that are made from a plant source, like soy, and are made to taste, and sometimes look, like animal proteins such as beef, chicken, duck, and pork. Some fake meats taste and feel very similar to the meat they are trying to imitate (and sometimes they really don't!). People who are vegetarian (see pages 39-40) eat only plant-based sources of protein and many include fake meats in their diets, as do many meat-eaters. However, it is important to remember that fake meats are processed foods, which means that they may contain a lot of additives (you will learn more about additives on page 78). Also, generally fake meats can be pretty expensive compared to other sources of protein.

While your body uses some of the protein you eat for energy (your carbs and fat supply the majority of energy to keep you going), your body mostly uses it to build. Just like bricks are put together to make a house, proteins are put together to make many parts of your body. Protein builds muscle (where most of the protein in your body can be found), hair, skin, bones, teeth, and nails. It can also be found in your major organs, like the brain, heart, liver, and kidneys. Protein is also vital when it comes to fighting off infections in the body.

Q: WHAT DOES IT MEAN TO BE VEGETARIAN?

A: Vegetarians do not eat foods that come from an animal, like a cow, a pig or a chicken. They may still drink cow's milk, eat cheese made from milk, and eat eggs. Some vegetarians also occasionally eat fish.

Q: WHY DO PEOPLE BECOME VEGETARIAN?

A: People choose to be vegetarian for many different reasons. Some of these include:
- Concern for the environment – it takes less energy to grow plant foods than raising animals for food[9];
- Disliking the thought of eating an animal that was once alive;
- Feeling healthier with mainly plant foods to eat;
- Religious reasons.

Q: CAN YOU BE A VEGETARIAN ONE DAY AND NOT ON OTHER DAYS?

A: You can eat a vegetarian lunch or supper one day, but that does not make you a vegetarian. Vegetarians make the decision to avoid eating meat altogether.

Q: SO WHAT EXACTLY DO YOU EAT WHEN YOU ARE A VEGETARIAN?

A: Vegetarians eat all sorts of fruits and vegetables (they will often eat more and a greater variety of these than non vegetarians!), grains, and cereals. Some may drink milk from cows, while others only drink soy milk, almond milk or rice milk. Instead of getting their protein from meat, they get protein from plant sources, such as soy (tofu), fake meats (see page 38), nuts and seeds, and legumes (like beans and chickpeas).

Q: Do vegetarians have trouble getting all the protein they need because they don't eat meat?

A: As long as they plan their meals carefully, vegetarians can get their daily requirements of protein from plant sources. However, it is important for vegetarians and meat-eaters alike to get their protein from a variety of sources.

Q: What about all of the other nutrients — do vegetarians get everything their bodies need?

A: Vegetarians can get all their nutrients by following a carefully planned, balanced vegetarian diet that includes lots of different fruits, vegetables, grains, and protein sources.

Q: What is tofu and is it really good for you?

A: Tofu is made from soybeans and water and is sold in the shape of a block. It comes in soft and firm varieties, and it has a nutty, kind of plain taste. When cooked with a sauce or with other foods, tofu actually takes on those other flavors, so it can be used in everything from dips, soups, and desserts, to a stir-fry, or a barbecue meal.

Tofu is a good source of protein, calcium, and iron. Many people who follow a vegetarian diet include tofu as a good plant-based source of protein, but it can also be a great part of non-vegetarian diets as well.

GIVE IT A TRY!

Here is a simple and delicious way you and your family can try tofu:

- 1 package firm tofu, cut into one-inch (2.5 cm) cubes
- 1/2 cup (125 mL) of your favorite stir-fry sauce, like honey garlic or peanut sauce

Put the tofu in a container with a lid. Pour the sauce over the tofu, put the lid on the container, and put it in the fridge. Leave the tofu to marinate for a minimum of one hour, and up to a maximum of one day. Be sure to flip your tofu at least once while it is marinating!

When you're ready, with an adult's help, heat a little olive oil or canola oil (about 1 Tbsp – 15 mL) in a large frying pan on the stove on medium-high heat. Empty the tofu and the sauce into the pan and cook for about five minutes, flipping the tofu cubes a

DID YOU KNOW?

NUTTY, CRUNCHY, YUMMY....MOTHS!?

That's right, **MOTHS.** Aborigines, who are the first people to ever live in Australia, ate moths regularly as a good source of protein.[10,11] Believe it or not, because moths have big muscles to fly, they are loaded with protein. And as a bonus, the fat that they have in their bodies is healthy, polyunsaturated fat! Some people say the insects are tastier raw after their wings are pulled off, while others enjoy them toasted and sprinkled on their food (YUM?).

In fact, in many parts of the world, people still eat all kinds of insects, such as termites, beetles, dragonflies, and ants as part of their regular diet. Insects can be prepared in many different ways, including boiled and mixed with coconut milk, garlic, and ginger, or even toasted and used to make bread.

Want to give these tasty treats a try? Check out your local zoo or science center. Many offer programs on bugs and insects, and some might even host special "bug tasting" events!

few times to make sure that they are heated through. Serve the tofu with wild rice and a vegetable like cooked broccoli or green beans. (YUM!)

Makes 4 servings.

One serving(1/2 cup or 125 mL) provides*:175 calories; 10.4 grams fat (16 % DV); 1.5 grams saturated fat (8 % DV); 0 mg cholesterol (0 % DV); 566 mg sodium (24 % DV); 14.6 grams protein; 8.9 grams carbohydrate (3 % DV); 2.2 grams fiber (9 % DV); 2.7 mg iron (19 % DV); 567 mg calcium (52 % DV); 134 IU vitamin A (4%DV); 0.2 mg vitamin C (0 % DV) *Approximate amounts; nutritional values may vary depending upon the type of sauce used.

Now generally, it is pretty easy to give your body the energy it needs from carbohydrate and fat every day. As for protein, it can be a little more tricky. Typically, there is not a lot of protein in snack foods (have you ever chomped on a steak at recess?), and sometimes we don't get enough protein-rich foods at our meals. What can make things a little stickier is that the nutrition facts on food labels often don't provide a % DV for protein. So, to help you get stocked with protein, here are three different food combos that, if spread throughout your day, will give you all the protein you need for one day:

1 chicken leg/thigh +
1 slice of whole wheat bread

or

2 cups (500 mL) milk +
1 egg +
2 slices of whole wheat bread +
1/2 oz (15 g) of sesame seeds

or

3 oz (90 g) of firm tofu +
2 Tbsp (25 mL) of nut butter +
2 slices of whole wheat bread +
1 cup (125 mL) of chickpeas +
1 cup (50 mL) of lentils

Did You Know?
Is Your Meat Kosher?

Some Jewish people choose to keep kosher for religious reasons. For meat to be considered kosher, it has to come from an animal with split hooves that chews its own cud, like a cow, a goat, or a lamb (cud is food that the animal has already chewed and swallowed that returns to the mouth to be chewed again for better digestion). Milk and milk products from kosher animals are okay for drinking and eating, but according to kosher law, milk and meat cannot be eaten together. Some birds, like chickens, turkeys, geese, and ducks are kosher as well. Both meat and poultry must be prepared according to kosher laws to be considered kosher.

Fish with fins and scales, such as salmon and halibut, are also kosher, but they require no special preparation.

So, what's not kosher? Meat from animals like pigs, horses, camels, and rabbits is not kosher, nor is the meat from shellfish, like shrimp and lobster.[12]

Moving On to Micros

Okay, before we move on, let's recap! Now you know that:

⊕ Food labels tell you what you need to know about what is in your food.

⊕ You get energy from the macronutrients in your food.

⊕ Complex carbs give you long-lasting energy.

⊕ Unsaturated fats are really good for you.

⊕ You can get protein from animal and plant foods.

Okay, you nutrient detectives, let's take an even closer at your food. There are tiny parts of your food that your body needs that are even smaller than the macronutrients. These are called the micronutrients.

CHAPTER

2

What's In Our Food Anyway?
Part II

micronutrients. They're smaller in size than the macros, and they don't provide your body with energy like the macros do. But does this mean that they are less important? No way! Each vitamin and mineral has a very specific and very important role to play in keeping your body healthy.

So, in this chapter, we are going to look at which specific foods are great sources of vitamins and minerals. And once you get to know the micros, you'll understand why you need to get a steady stream of them every day.

47

CHECK THE LABEL

Let's go back to the food label. We know that we can find the macronutrient listings on the top of the label, but let's take a look at the bottom. Here is where we find information about which micronutrients are in the food we eat (except for sodium, which is with the macros at the top of the label).

Micronutrients are very, very small parts of food, but despite their small size, they make big things happen! They regulate and manage many of the normal functions of your body, like growth, healing, and the movement of your muscles. Both vitamins and minerals are considered micronutrients.

Our bodies only need a small amount of vitamins and minerals every day to stay healthy. In fact, micronutrients are typically measured in milligrams, International Units, and micrograms. However, nutrition labels measure micros in % Daily Value (remember that from page 19? — we'll go over it again later in this chapter).

Nutrition Facts

Serving Size 1 cup (228g)
Servings Per Container 2

Amount Per Serving	
Calories 250	Calories from Fat 110

	% Daily Value*
Total Fat 12g	18%
Saturated Fat 3g	15%
Trans Fat 1.5g	
Cholesterol 30mg	10%
Sodium 470mg	20%
Total Carbohydrate 31g	10%
Dietary Fiber 0g	0%
Sugars 5g	
Protein 5g	

Vitamin A	4%
Vitamin C	2%
Calcium	20%
Iron	4%

* Percent Daily Values are based on a 2,000 calorie diet. Your Daily Values may be higher or lower depending on your calorie needs:

	Calories:	2,000	2,500
Total Fat	Less than	65g	80g
Sat Fat	Less than	20g	25g
Cholesterol	Less than	300mg	300mg
Sodium	Less than	2,400mg	2,400mg
Total Carbohydrate		300g	375g
Dietary Fiber		25g	30g

Source: U.S. Food and Drug Administration (FDA)

A NOTE ABOUT FOOD LABELS:

In North America, food manufacturers have to include the calories and amounts of fat, cholesterol, sodium, carbohydrates, proteins, vitamins A and C, iron, and calcium per serving on the food label. They will only include other vitamins or minerals on their label if their food is a "source" of a particular micronutrient (food manufacturers like to brag about how healthy their foods are!).

So, for example, if you're wondering if a serving of a particular food is a good source of vitamin D, check the nutrition label. If it is there, it will tell you what % of your Daily Value is in one serving of that food. If you don't see vitamin D on the label, then you can bet that a serving of that food is not a good source of D.

Did You Know?

How small is a microgram? Think about it this way: A penny weighs three grams. If you break a penny into 5,000 smaller pieces, each of those pieces weighs 600 micrograms. That is about how much vitamin A you need every day!

You can find micronutrients in tiny amounts in almost all of the food groups. However, when it comes to certain vitamins and minerals, we do know that particular food groups can be considered main suppliers:

➔ You can get vitamin C from many (but not all) fruits and vegetables.

➔ You're almost guaranteed to get a good supply of calcium from milk and milk products.

➔ You can get your B vitamins, iron, and zinc from most breads, cereals, rice, and pasta.

Vital Vitamins

A vitamin is a tiny chemical that is found in plants and animals. There are 13 main vitamins, each with its own structure – some are quite simple structures while others are more complex. Despite their differences, all vitamins are part of the many processes that go on in your body. In fact, they help your body use macros properly: they help make carbohydrates and fats into energy that the body can use, and they help protein make bones and tissues that the body needs to grow and stay healthy.

Q: Do I need to take a vitamin pill every day to stay healthy?

A: No. If you eat a variety of different foods, you do not need to take vitamin pills to stay healthy. Many kids and adults take vitamin pills because it's sort of like insurance that they are getting all the vitamins they need, in case they do not eat a completely balanced diet. Unfortunately, some people believe that vitamin pills actually replace food – but they DON'T!

The exception is when someone has a medical or health reason that makes them need more of some vitamins and minerals. If you have a medical condition, it is smart to check with your doctor to see if you do need to take vitamin and mineral supplements.

INSTANT HISTORY FACTS

A BIT(E) OF VITAMIN HISTORY

About 3500 years ago: The importance of vitamins was first discovered in Egypt. A physician squeezed the juice out of a dead animal's liver and realized that when his patient drank the juice, his night blindness was cured.[1] A few years later, in 400 B.C.E., a famous Greek physician named Hippocrates also figured out that eating ox liver dipped in honey could cure night blindness. Though neither doctor knew it at the time, both of them had found concentrated sources of vitamin A![2]

In the 1700s, sailors who were on long voyages did not eat enough fruits and vegetables. Many of them developed scurvy, a condition that makes a person's skin very pale, causes their gums to bleed, and makes their teeth fall out. Some sailors even died of scurvy. It was later discovered that the condition was caused by a lack of vitamin C. So when the sailors ate more citrus fruits, like limes, lemons, and oranges, they didn't need to worry about scurvy![3]

In the late 1800s, people started moving from their farms in the country to work in factories in the cities. After living in the city for a while, many kids' bones were weakening, and even bending! They were diagnosed with a condition called rickets, which we now know is caused by a deficiency of vitamin D.

Why were these kids okay in the country but had this problem in the city? Well, when they lived in the country, kids worked and played out in open fields in the sunshine, which we know is a great source of vitamin D for our bodies. When they moved to the city, kids could only play in dark, narrow alleys, so they couldn't get the sun they needed.[4] Also, conditions in cities at that time were very poor, and many kids did not have a range of healthy foods to choose from. Unfortunately, rickets is a condition that still happens today.[5]

Vitamins fit into one of two groups: some are in the fat-soluble group and the others are in the water-soluble group. The fat-soluble vitamins – vitamins A, D, E, and K – dissolve in fat and are absorbed in the intestines along with fat in our food. Fat-soluble vitamins can be stored in your body's organs (like the liver and kidney) and in fat tissue all over your body for a while, but not for too long. That is why you need to have a new supply every day. How do these vitamins get out of storage and put to use? They are transported out or they make their own way to where they are needed. When your body needs vitamin A, for example, a protein from the liver carries it out – sort of like a piggyback ride – and to your eyes, where the vitamin helps you see.

Water-soluble vitamins dissolve in water, so they get absorbed in the intestines on their own. The water-soluble vitamins are the B vitamins and vitamin C. Because they are water-soluble, it means they cannot be stored in the body like the fat-soluble ones. Once your body uses what it needs of these water-soluble vitamins, it gets rid of them by flushing them out in your pee.

WHERE ARE THEY?

Your body needs to get most vitamins from the foods you eat (except for a couple of vitamins that your body can make for itself). Let's see where we can find them!

VITAMIN A

Think of vitamin A as the seeing and protecting vitamin. Vitamin A keeps your eyes healthy. It also makes sure your bones develop normally and keeps your skin healthy, which protects you from getting infections.

This vitamin can be found in milk and cheese, and in protein sources like liver and eggs. It can also be found in some fruits and vegetables, like mangoes, apricots, carrots, sweet potatoes, and pumpkins. In fact, there is a special form of vitamin A in these foods that gives them their yellow and orange color. It is called carotene, which is a carotenoid.

Did You Know?

For kids who have regular access to a good variety of foods, vitamin A deficiency is not really a concern. However, when kids don't have easy access to foods like spinach, carrots, or meats, they may not be getting all the vitamin A they need. In fact, according to an organization called Unite for Sight, a lack of vitamin A is the leading preventable cause of blindness among children around the world.[6]

Fast Bite

Mellow Yellow

Not that long ago, farmers discovered that when they fed their hogs white corn, their hogs got sick. And yet, when they fed the hogs yellow corn, the hogs got better. Can you guess the reason? Yellow corn had the vitamin A carotenoid, which the hogs needed to get in their diet.[7] Even hogs need their vitamins!

Q: WHAT DO FLAMINGOS, SALMON, AND COOKED LOBSTERS ALL HAVE IN COMMON?

A: Carotenoids! They each get their bright color from the carotenoid-rich plants that they have eaten to stay healthy.[8] (Tidbit: live lobsters are greenish brown or blue, which also comes from the food they eat. When a lobster is cooked, the heat releases the carotenoids and the lobster turns a YUMmy shade of pink).

GET YOUR DAILY DOSE!

Here are easy, tasty ways to be sure that you get your A every day:

→ Make carrots and tomatoes a healthy school snack.

→ Add chopped apricots to a muffin recipe.

→ Add mango slices to your fruit smoothie.

VITAMIN B

Think of the B vitamins as a team. This team is made up of eight players called thiamin (vitamin B1), riboflavin (vitamin B2), pyridoxine (vitamin B 6), niacin, biotin, folate, pantothenic acid, and cobalmin (B 12). The main purpose of all of the B vitamins is to help your body cells make energy out of your broken-down macronutrients and to help your cells to use that energy to get stuff done.

Good food sources of the team of Bs are protein sources, including meats, fish, chicken, eggs, and legumes. Also, breakfast cereals are often fortified with the B vitamins thiamin, niacin, and riboflavin.

Did You Know?

Be sure to get your Bs

When you see your favorite athletes, you probably think they must be pretty healthy and that they eat well in order to perform well in their sports. But it turns out that some athletes might actually not be getting enough of the B vitamins[9], which help the body use proteins for building and repairing tissues, and use sugars and fats for energy. If athletes have a poor diet on top of this lack of Bs, then they may not do as well at their sports as they could. What can you do if you play sports? Make sure you get enough Bs!

Get Your Daily Dose!

Try these tips to get your fill of Bs:

⊖ Eat whole grains, dark green veggies, nuts, meats, and dairy foods.

⊖ Add chicken to a bowl of brown rice.

⊖ Have scrambled eggs for breakfast or supper.

⊖ Eat low-sugar cereals that are fortified with the Bs.

Vitamin C

Vitamin C is the structural and healing vitamin. C helps to build bones and cartilage, which is found in the tip of your nose, in your ears, and other places. When food manufacturers want to add C to their food, they add ascorbic acid to the product, which will appear in the list of ingredients on the food's packaging.

The best sources of vitamin C are fruits and vegetables, like kiwis, oranges, grapefruits, lemons, papayas, cantaloupes, mangoes, strawberries, broccoli, tomatoes, and green peppers (YUM!).

Q: DOES VITAMIN C REALLY CURE A COLD?

A: Scientists do not know for sure, but probably not. Vitamin C might make your cold last for a shorter time by helping your body fight the virus that causes the sneezes and runny nose of a cold.[10] The idea that vitamin C could prevent colds was first proposed in the 1970s by a man named Linus Pauling, a Nobel-prize winning chemist who did a lot of work with vitamin C.[11]

So what *can* you do to get rid of a cold? Get lots of rest. What can you do to avoid spreading your cold germs to other people (and even prevent other people from giving you their cold germs)? Wash your hands with soap, often: before you eat, when you come home from school, after sports. And be sure to wash them long enough — you should be able to say the alphabet slowly as you soap up your hands with warm water. Then rinse your hands thoroughly and dry them on a clean towel.

GET YOUR DAILY DOSE!

Get your C with these tricks:

⊖ Cut up kiwis and mangoes and have them as a snack or with your lunch.

⊖ Add oranges to your spinach salad.

⊖ Add sliced tomatoes to your sandwiches.

All quick and easy ways to get your vitamin C!

VITAMIN D

Vitamin D is added to milk and is found naturally in protein-rich foods, like beef and chicken liver, eggs, salmon, trout, herring, tuna, and sardines (YUM!). What's one of the best sources of vitamin D? Look up! When the sun's rays contact your skin, your body actually creates vitamin D. So, we can think of vitamin D as the sunshine vitamin.

Did You Know?

To get the right amount of sunshine for your body to make vitamin D, you need to expose your arms and legs to direct sunlight for at least 10 to 20 minutes, three to four times per week. Now, the problem here is that your skin can't be covered with sunscreen for this absorption to happen, so you need to be really careful and consult with an adult before you give this a try. Also, in northern cities, like Boston and Toronto, the rays from the sun in winter are not strong enough to let your body make vitamin D – so there's no use standing around in the snow in your T-shirt and shorts trying to catch those rays![12]

Q: CAN YOU GET VITAMIN D THROUGH THE CAR WINDOW?

A: No. Rays from the sun that help you make vitamin D don't go through windows. In fact, in many large cities, polluted air acts like a window and blocks a lot of the important rays that your body needs.[13, 14]

DID YOU KNOW?

REPTILES: SUN-BATHING BEAUTIES?

If you have a reptile as a pet, make sure that it is getting enough direct exposure to sunlight. Animals like snakes, turtles, and lizards do not get enough vitamin D from the food they eat. This means that they need some sun exposure to make their D.

If bringing your pet outside every day is not a reasonable option (and remember, sunlight through the window doesn't count!), you can buy a special light for them that imitates the sun's rays. Otherwise, your pet can get really weak bones – imagine, a reptile with rickets![15]

GET YOUR DAILY DOSE!

Try these i-**D**-eas:
- Put canned sardines on light rye bread for a tasty snack.
- Add cooked salmon to a lettuce salad with a nice low-salt soy dressing.
- Mix cooked egg into your wild rice dish.
- Let your body get some sun when you can.

Vitamin E

Your cells are where all of the action happens in your body: energy is stored, energy is released, and cells die and are created. During all of these processes, some waste material is created. When it is floating around inside your body, this "body garbage" can cause a lot of damage to your cells. Vitamin E helps to clean up all of that garbage. That's why vitamin E can be called the janitor vitamin. Vitamin E also increases the activity of antibodies, which are special proteins that help fight off infections. The group of vitamins and chemicals that perform these clean-up jobs are also called antioxidants.

The best source of vitamin E is a cereal called wheat germ, or the oil that comes from wheat germ. However, it can also be found in other grains, and in many oils, like corn oil, olive oil, and soybean oil. Nuts like almonds, peanuts, and pistachios also have vitamin E, and even mangoes contain some E.

GET YOUR DAILY DOSE!

You can get your E with these tips:

→ Eat foods that have been prepared with vegetable oils like corn oil or olive oil.

→ When cooking scrambled eggs, use a mixture of butter and olive oil instead of butter alone.

→ Add wheat germ to homemade pancake mixes, cookies, bars, and cereals.

→ Add chopped almonds and pistachios to your bowl of ice cream for a vitamin E boost.

FAST BITE

Dark chocolate is actually a source of antioxidants that help keep blood healthy. However, before you buy the entire supply of chocolate bars at your corner store, be sure to get "dark" chocolate because the milk in "milk" chocolate prevents your body from absorbing some of the antioxidants (check for "dark chocolate" or "70% cocoa" or higher on the label). Also, because chocolate can be high in calories, try to eat it in small quantities.

Vitamin K

There is no such thing as vitamin F, vitamin G, vitamin H, vitamin I, or vitamin J. However, the is vitamin K, the bandage vitamin! When you cut yourself, this vitamin helps your blood to cl and make a scab that stops the bleeding.

You can get vitamin K from many vegetables, like spinach, broccoli, kale, cabbage, cau flower, and darker lettuces like romaine. It can also be found in protein-rich soybeans, and ir some cereals. The trillions of bugs that are in your intestines (which you will read about in the next chapter) also make vitamin K for your body.

Get Your Daily Dose!

All of these will give you some K, OK?
→ Mix lightly cooked broccoli with cold whole wheat noodles for a refreshing, tasty salad.
→ Try edamame (soy beans - YUM!) as a snack (squeeze the beans out of their pods).
→ Use romaine lettuce in your next egg salad sandwich.

MARVELOUS MINERALS

A mineral is part of the earth that then becomes part of animals and plants. There are over 20 different minerals, each with their own unique structure. In addition to small amounts of vitamins, your body also needs small amounts of minerals. Like vitamins, minerals make sure the processes in your body are going smoothly. However, minerals also ensure that your blood carries oxygen, that your bones and teeth are strong, and that your body fluids are balanced.

We will look at certain minerals that are especially important to your body, such as calcium, iron, zinc, potassium, and sodium.

Did you Know?

Believe it or not, your body is made up of about three pounds (1 1/2 kg) of minerals. Of those three pounds, one pound (1/2 kg) is calcium. In comparison, iron makes up only about 0.07 ounces (2.0 grams), or 2/3 of the weight of a penny.[16] Despite their size difference, both minerals are crucial to having a healthy body.

Calcium

Calcium is the bone and tooth mineral because it makes up the structure of these parts of your body. Small amounts of this mineral are also needed to heal a cut and to keep your muscles moving, which includes getting your heart to pump blood to all parts of your body.

Calcium is found in milk and dairy products; some sources of protein, like sardines, legumes, and tofu; some nuts and seeds, like almonds and sesame seeds; and broccoli. Plant beverages like soy milk, almond milk, and rice milk, and orange juice are often fortified with calcium (for more information on adding vitamins and minerals to food see page 77).

Fast Bite

When vitamin D gets into your bloodstream, it sends out signals to your intestines to let calcium into your bloodstream too. This is why it is important to eat a calcium source with a source of vitamin D. It works out well that foods like milk and sardines both contain vitamin D and calcium. But for other calcium-rich foods, like broccoli and almonds, you'll need to have a source of D with them, like eggs or a glass of milk, to ensure that you will get all the calcium your body needs.

Did You Know?

BANKING ON CALCIUM

Not only does your body use calcium to build your bones – it also stores calcium in your bones. When you are in your 20s and 30s, your body will start to use a lot of the calcium that is stored in your bones. So, it's really important that you get a lot of calcium when you are young so that you have lots saved up in your bone bank for later![17]

Get Your Daily Dose!

Eat all of these and you'll get all the calcium you need in one day:

→ 1/2 cup (125 mL) 2 % milk + 1 cup (250 mL) vanilla yogurt + fruits (see smoothie recipe on page 120)

→ 1 cup (250 mL) cream of broccoli soup

→ 1/2 cup (125 mL) almonds

→ 1 cup (250 mL) ice cream

→ 1 ounce (30 g) cheese

Iron

Iron is the strong mineral because it makes sure that your body gets the oxygen it needs. By clinging to a particular kind of protein that is found in your blood, iron brings oxygen from the air that you breathe to cells all over your body.

Iron is found in protein sources like meat, chicken, fish, tofu, beans, and lentils. It can also be found in fruits and vegetables, like dried apricots and raisins, spinach, and broccoli, and in fortified breads and cereals.

Fast Bite

As you can see, iron and calcium are found in all types of different foods, but many kids in North America just aren't getting enough of these important minerals every day.[18] One main reason is that salty and sugary snacks, soda pop, and juice are replacing fruits and vegetables in kids' diets. So be sure to pay special attention to the foods you know have iron and calcium.

Fast Bite

Plant-based sources of iron, like beans, soy products, and dried fruit, have a different form of iron than the iron found in animal-based foods, like meat and chicken. Your body needs a little extra help from vitamin C to use plant-based iron. So, when you eat iron-rich plant foods like tofu or raisins, it's a good idea to also eat a veggie or a fruit that is a good source of vitamin C, like green peppers, oranges, or strawberries (YUM!), so that your body gets the iron it needs.

GET YOUR DAILY DOSE!

Make sure that you get enough iron by including iron-rich foods in at least two meals every day. Here is an example of how you can get the iron you need each day:

1/2 cup (125 mL) oatmeal with 1 Tbsp (15 mL) raisins +
1/2 cup (125 mL) chili +
1 chicken breast +
1/2 cup (125 mL) spinach

or, for vegetarians:

1/2 cup (125 mL) oatmeal with 1 Tbsp (15 mL) raisins +
1/2 cup (125 mL) chili
1/2 cup (125 mL) firm tofu
2 Tbsp (25 mL) of cashew butter
1/2 cup (125 mL) spinach
(Remember that iron from plant sources should be eaten with a source of vitamin C, like strawberries or oranges.)

IRON ON THE BRAIN

Your brain needs a constant supply of oxygen or it doesn't work properly. If you don't get enough iron, it's much more difficult for the oxygen to travel to your brain, where it's needed. If this happens, you'll feel tired, crabby, and it might even cause you to get sick because iron also helps you to fight off infections. So be sure to pump up your iron every day!

Zinc

Zinc is the smelling and tasting mineral. Zinc can be found in milk and cheese; cereals and grains, including wheat germ and whole grain bread; and in protein sources, like beef, turkey, and nuts.

Zinc is a busy mineral. Zinc helps keep the hair on your head and it helps you heal after you get a cut or scrape. You need zinc to grow, fight infections, and heal your wounds. But probably the most popular job of zinc? To make sure you can taste and smell. Because of zinc, you are able to detect the wonderful stir-fry cooking in the kitchen (YUM!) and the sweet scent of grass after the rain. Zinc is a part of gustin. Gustin? That's a protein that is found in your saliva that helps you taste the food that you are eating. So, the next time you lick that chocolate ice cream, you have zinc to thank for that delicious taste!

Get Your Daily Dose!

Try these tips to get your zinc:

→ Add cheese to your vegetable soup.

→ Mix nuts in with your oatmeal.

→ Make sure you get some protein with each meal.

POTASSIUM AND SODIUM

Potassium and sodium are two minerals that are very similar: they both keep body fluids in check, which is why they're known as regulators (or traffic controllers!). They also are part of the activity of your nerve cells – the cells that make you feel pain or tickles.

Potassium acts like a pump in cell walls, letting certain substances in and out of the cell. Potassium also helps to make your muscles work, so that you can swing a hockey stick or hit a home run. You can get potassium from protein sources like meats, chicken, and fish, and also from a wide variety of fruits and vegetables, including bananas, avocados, cantaloupes, apricots, oranges, kiwis, spinach, tomatoes, and potatoes.

Like potassium, sodium also acts like a pump in the walls of cells, to ensure that certain chemicals get in while others can get out. The body is made up of fluids, and sodium helps to keep the fluids balanced.

A common source of sodium is table salt. It can also be found in many processed foods, like hot dogs, cold cuts, ham, and bacon; in salty snacks, like chips, pretzels, popcorn, and crackers; in fast foods, like hamburgers and sandwiches; and in condiments, like soy sauce, ketchup, and some salad dressings. It's also found in cheese.

Did You Know?

Kids and adults are getting about two times the amount of salt that their bodies need, and many people are getting even more than that.[19,20] Too much salt on food over a long period of time makes your heart work harder than it should (it is good to have your heart work harder when you are exercising, but when this ongoing hard work is caused by sodium, it can cause a lot of problems).

Q: Why are we getting so much salt?

A: Many people in North America eat a lot of junk food, which is loaded with salt. Also, most manufacturers add salt to their processed foods to bump up the flavor. Even recipes for cookies, brownies, and cupcakes call for a little salt to be added to make the flavors pop. And think about it: what are the two most common things to add to your food? Salt and pepper!

In fact, people can get so used to the taste of salt that they often need more and more to be able to taste their food properly.

There are tons of ways to make sure that you're not getting too much sodium in your diet. Here are just a few ideas:

⊖ Choose snacks that have no salt, like fruits and vegetables, or homemade foods where you can control the amount of salt used, like homemade soup and cookies.

⊖ Try sprinkling lemon or lime juice on your food for added flavor, or try black pepper, or different dried or fresh herbs, like oregano, basil, and parsley.

⊖ Eat corn on the cob (YUM!) without the salt and butter. Corn is so sweet that you'll probably find that it's delicious on its own.

⊖ Use less ketchup and soy sauce on the food you eat.

⊖ Try to keep store-prepared pizzas, sandwiches, hamburgers, and hot dogs to a minimum – this is where most people are getting all their salt.

⊖ Remove the salt shaker from the dinner table.

⊖ In the grocery store, check out the amount of sodium in a serving of the different foods available to you. Try to choose the products with less sodium as often as possible.

Q: WAIT A MINUTE! SODIUM IS A MICRONUTRIENT, BUT IT'S LISTED ON MY NUTRITION LABEL WITH THE MACRONUTRIENTS. WHAT GIVES?

A: Because people are generally concerned about how much sodium they get, the people who create these labels have decided that sodium needs to be closer to the top of the list, so people don't miss it.

now that you know about the major nutrient players in your food, let's take another look at that nutrition label and figure out which foods are nutrient powerhouses, and which foods are not.

When you look at the bottom half of a nutrition label, you'll see that next to each micronutrient, there is a percentage. Do you remember what that's all about? We already talked about % Daily Value on page 19, but here's a quick refresher: if you take a test and you get everything right, you get 100%. So, if a food label tells you that one serving of that food contains 50% of your Daily Value of calcium, you know that you have about half of the calcium you need for that day. That serving of food is a good source of calcium, but remember that you'll still need to get more calcium from other foods for that day.

But, unlike a math test, you cannot get 100% of all of the macro and micro nutrients you need from one food. There is no such thing as one perfect food. This is why you need to mix it up and eat lots of different foods so that you get at least 100 % of all of your nutrients.

Remember that a serving of food that gives you 15% or more of a nutrient is a good source of that nutrient. If that serving gives you less than 15% of a nutrient, it is not a good source of that nutrient. This holds true for both your macronutrients and your micronutrients.[21, 22]

MICROS FOR ALL

The Micronutrient Initiative is a Canadian-based charity that has only one goal: to put a stop to vitamin and mineral deficiencies around the world. They work with people in over 75 countries to fortify foods with vitamin A, iodine, iron, and zinc to keep both kids and adults healthy. Their website is http://www.micronutrient.org.

Let's take a look at a real food label and see if it is a good source of macronutrients and micronutrients.

This is a label from the grain quinoa.

ASK YOURSELF:

What size is the serving?

What about carbs?

What about fiber?

What about fat?

What about protein?

So, is one serving of quinoa a good source of macros?

Is it a good source of vitamins A and C?

Is it a good source of calcium and iron?

What about sodium?

Does the label list any other micros?

So, is one serving a good source of micros?

Do you think this is a healthy choice for you?

(Turn the page to see how you did!)

Nutrition Facts

Serving Size 1/4 Cup uncooked (45g)
Servings Per Container about 10

Amount Per Serving

Calories 180	Calories from Fat 35

	% Daily Value*
Total Fat 3.5g	**5%**
Saturated Fat 0g	**0%**
Trans Fat 0g	
Cholesterol 0mg	**0%**
Sodium 10mg	**0%**
Potassium 260mg	**7%**
Total Carbohydrate 29g	**10%**
Dietary Fiber 11g	**44%**
Sugars 2g	
Protein 7g	**12%**

Vitamin A 4%	•	Calcium 2%
Iron 15%	•	Vitamin E 10%
Thiamin B1 6%	•	Riboflavin B2 15%
Folate 4%	•	Phosphorus 25%
Magnesium 15%	•	Zinc 15%

Not a significant source of vitamin C
*Percent Daily Values are based on a 2,000 calorie diet.

Courtesy of Eden Foods

Okay, so the quinoa label on the previous page tells us the following information:

What size is the serving? 1/4 c (45 g)
What about carbs? 10 %
What about fiber?   44 %
What about fat? 5 %
What about protein? 12 %

Is one serving of this quinoa a source of macros? *It is a source of fiber and protein.*

Is it a source of vitamins A and C? *Not a significant source.*

Is it a source of calcium and iron? *Not a significant source of calcium (2 %), but it is a source of iron (15 %)*

What about sodium? 0 %

Is this serving a good source of any other micros? *Yes, B2: 15%, phosphorus: 25%, magnesium 15%, zinc 15%*

Is one serving of this quinoa a source of micros? *Yes, it is a source of minerals.*

So, do you think this quinoa is a healthy choice for you? By now, you are probably saying, "Yes, I do, because no one food is going to give me 100% of what I need. But this one serving of quinoa will give me lots of fiber and some protein, with quite a variety of minerals. Nice!"

Try quinoa mixed with some veggies. Try it for breakfast with vanilla yogurt and some seeds sprinkled over the top (YUM!).

BABY CARROTS: VITAMIN A POWERHOUSES!

According to the label on a bag of baby carrots, a serving size is eight carrots. But farther down on the label, you'll see that those eight carrots give you 172% of the vitamin A that you need in one day. That's some powerful produce! But baby carrots are not really a good source of any other micros. Nobody's perfect!

Now you know about some of the vitamins and minerals that are really important to your health. Sometimes, when certain vitamins and minerals are missing from packaged foods, manufacturers add them in to make your food even healthier. But sometimes they add other chemicals, which don't make them healthier at all. Read on!

To Add or Not to Add, That is the Question!

What does it mean when a food is labeled "enriched"? When a food is enriched, it means that the manufacturer has added vitamins or minerals to make it healthier. Government organizations that are in charge of a country's health issues try to keep track of which micronutrients their citizens are missing in their daily diets. When they notice this happening, they tell food manufacturers to add certain quantities of certain nutrients to foods to make sure that people get what they need. In the past, iodine (a mineral) has been added to table salt, vitamin D has been added to milk and soymilk, and B vitamins have been added to cereals.

Another reason that manufacturers enrich their food is that nutrients can be lost when certain ingredients are used in a food product. For example, food companies often use white flour for their foods. This means that the healthy outer layer of the wheat grain was removed, which leaves the white core of the grain to make flour. When this happens, the food companies often add vitamins and minerals to the white flour to "enrich" it. This flour will appear as "enriched flour" in the food's list of ingredients.

Enriching foods can be a really good thing, especially when people are generally not getting enough of a certain nutrient. However, doesn't it make a lot more sense to eat foods that don't need to be enriched, like fruits, vegetables, and whole grains? They're naturally rich with nutrients! While eating "enriched" foods is good for you, eating foods with other chemicals added to them is not so good for your health.

Some food companies also add chemicals to prevent harmful bacteria from growing on their food, because they want their packaged food to stay "fresh" for a really long time. This means that their foods can stay on grocery store shelves longer than if they did not have the chemicals. These are called additives.

Years ago when people did not have refrigerators and freezers to keep their food fresh, some of these chemicals were really useful. But now that most people have these appliances in their homes, it makes a lot more sense to buy and eat fresh food with no additives, like fresh fruits and vegetables, fresh or frozen fish, chicken, and meat. And why add chemicals to your food to make it taste better – why not eat fresh foods that naturally taste great?

Q: IF I'M CRAVING SOMETHING SWEET, CAN I EAT "DIET" FOODS THAT CONTAIN ALMOST NO CALORIES?

A: You can, but you should try to keep them to a minimum because they don't provide you with much energy. Artificial sweeteners are like fake sugar, and are added to foods to make them sweeter, without adding any calories. Some common artificial sweeteners are aspartame, sucralose, or cyclamate. As you learned on page 31, people who are diabetic cannot use carbohydrates without insulin, so "diet" foods that have artificial sweeteners in them, like diet soft drinks, diet hot chocolate mixes, and diet cookies, can be a real treat for them.

Also, as you will learn on page 105, diet foods can send your body mixed signals about your hunger and whether or not you're full. So, it really is a good idea to not eat too much fake sugar.

FAST BITE

MSG: AN ADDITIVE TO WATCH OUT FOR!
MSG, or monosodium glutamate, is an additive that is used to enhance or pick up the flavor in certain foods. Generally, foods with MSG also contain lots of sodium. You might find MSG in many fast food items, as well as in some canned soups and frozen meals. If you're eating a lot of fresh-tasting fruits and vegetables often, you will be limiting your MSG intake already. However, keep your eyes peeled for MSG in the ingredient list of foods, and try to limit eating those foods.

Make the choice to keep processed, packaged, non-fresh foods, like canned pastas, salty crackers, cheese and processed meat snacks, to a minimum in your diet. Load up on fresh foods more often and you'll be all set!

Micros are magnificent, even in minute amounts! I guess good things do come in small packages (except for those additives!).

Now that you know all kinds of stuff about micros, macros, and how food labels work, you can officially consider yourself a label-reading pro. Congratulations! And now that you're so savvy, you've got to use what you know to make healthy choices to ensure that your body is getting exactly what it needs.

PUTTING IT ALL TOGETHER

Okay, let's recap! After reading this chapter, you now know that:

⊕ Micronutrients (vitamins and minerals) manage many functions in your body.

⊕ You need to get your vitamins: A (seeing and protecting vitamin), B (team vitamin), C (structural and healing vitamin), D (sunshine vitamin), E (janitor vitamin), and K (bandage vitamin).

⊕ You need to get your minerals: calcium (bone and tooth mineral), iron (strong mineral), zinc (smelling and tasting mineral), and potassium and sodium (traffic controller minerals).

⊕ Your body is getting what it needs when a serving of food has at least 15% of your Daily Value of some macros and micros.

⊕ Enriched foods are okay, especially if they give you nutrients that you're missing.

⊕ It's a good idea to avoid additives, like MSG and fake sugars, as much as possible.

So, let's look at just how your body takes the food you eat and turns it into stuff that it can use. Read on to discover how your body decides when it's time to eat and drink, how food gets digested and absorbed, and how this all affects your body's balance of energy in and energy out.

CHAPTER

3

THE AMAZING BODY

ow that you've read about what's in your food, from the larger macros to the smaller micros, you have a pretty good idea about why foods that are "nutrient rich" are really good for you.

So, let's find out how your body gets these nutrients from the food you eat, how your body turns certain nutrients into energy, and how to keep your body in balance.

You have probably heard many times that "you are what you eat." But is this really true? Does food really become part of your body? Read on to find out!

CUE DIGESTION

RRRRING! The school bell rings, everyone puts their work away and gets their lunch, or gets in line at the cafeteria. All of these are signals that it's lunchtime. There are also more complicated signals that happen outside and inside your body that tell your brain: "Get ready! It's chow time!"

HUNGER CUES

As you sit down to that supper of amazing grilled fish with mango salsa and brown rice (YUM!), your digestive system has already started to work. That's because the delicious sights and smells of your meal signal to your brain that it's time to eat. Also, things like your mood and the levels of sugar, fat, and protein in your blood send messages to your brain and affect whether or not you are ready to eat.

Once your brain knows that it is time to eat, it sends out messages to different parts of your digestive system to get ready for the incoming food: saliva begins to flow in your mouth and digestive juices are released in your stomach and in your intestines. Gases in your intestines can create a funny gurgling noise when you're hungry.

Another important message sent to your brain is the level of sugar, fat, and protein in your blood. If any of these levels are low, then your brain knows that you need to eat more to fuel your body.

THIRST CUES

There is a similar kind of signaling system that tells you when you're thirsty. Obviously, a dry mouth is a signal from your body to drink more water.

Also, when you have enough fluids, your urine should be a pale or light yellow and you should be peeing at least a couple of times a day. However, if your body is not getting enough fluids, your pee will be a darker color, like the color of apple juice, and you won't pee that often.

If you can, drink water about every 1 – 2 hours (approximately 4 oz. – 6 oz. / 120 – 180 mL) to give your body the fluid it needs.

Did You Know?

HUNGRY VS. THIRSTY
Sometimes you might think that you're hungry, when actually, you're thirsty. This can lead to a lot of unnecessary snacking. The next time you're unsure about your signals, have a drink of water and wait a few minutes. If you are still hungry, then have a healthy snack.

Q&A:
BODY OF WATER

Q: How much water do I need to keep my body healthy?

A: Your body is about 60% water[1] – that's more than half of your entire body! Water is an important part of your blood; it keeps your organs, like your liver and kidneys, in good shape; and your body flushes out some of the stuff it doesn't need in your pee, which is mostly made of water. So, you need to drink about 4-6 cups (1 to 1.5 L) of water every day, depending on your activity level. You will get extra water by eating fruits and veggies, by having soup, and by drinking milk.

Q: Do I need to drink more fluids when I do sports?

A: Absolutely! In fact, not only do you need more water, but you also need a little bit more sodium (you can find out more about this mineral on page 71). When you exercise, your body sweats to keep cool, and sweat is made of water and sodium, which is why sweat tastes salty. Try drinking about 1 - 2 cups (250 to 500 mL) of water a couple of hours before your activity starts. It's also a good idea to have a serving of salted whole grain crackers, or salted pretzels, to give you a little extra sodium.

Once you start, try having 1/2 cup (125 mL) of water every twenty minutes or so while you are active. Keep in mind that if you are exercising outside on a hot day, or if you live in a really warm place, you might need even more water (and salty foods) to keep your body balanced.[2]

Q: I'VE HEARD THAT A CAMEL'S HUMP STORES WATER. IS THAT TRUE?

A. **Nope. In fact, a camel's hump is loaded with fat, not water. The camel uses its fat reserves to make some water and for energy, just like you (find out more about how that works on page 99).**

Camels don't really sweat that much, so they're really good at saving up the water that is in their bodies. Because of this, camels are used to help people travel long distances in the desert. On these travels, people need to bring food and water for themselves, but they do not need to bring much for their camel. This means that traveling with a camel is relatively easy.

The camel can go for weeks without drinking. But when that camel gets thirsty – watch out! It can drink up to 450 cups (112 L) within 10 to 15 minutes![3]

DIGESTION

When you eat, your food takes a ride down one very long tunnel that has many different parts. This is called your digestive tract. At different points on its ride, your food changes speeds – at some points, it moves through really quickly, while at other points it is incredibly slow. Along the way, it's broken apart into smaller and smaller pieces until it is so tiny, it can be absorbed into your bloodstream. Once those nutrients enter your cells, they are used for energy, for building body structures, or for regulating all kinds of body functions. So let's follow a cheese sandwich on whole grain bread through your digestive tract to see what happens!

First, your front teeth help you take that first bite of the sandwich. Your side teeth and your molars get in on the action and chew the bread and cheese into smaller pieces. Saliva is released into your mouth, which starts breaking up the complex carbs in the bread and turning them into simple sugars. Saliva also dissolves some of the bread and cheese so that the taste buds on your tongue can taste the salty cheese and the nutty bread (YUM!). Your saliva also contains chemicals that keep your teeth clean.

RIDDLE

THERE ARE 10,000 OF THEM AND WE GET NEW ONES EVERY 2 WEEKS! WHAT ARE THEY?

Answer: Taste buds. Taste buds are the tiny little bumps on your tongue that help you taste foods that are salty, sour, bitter, sweet, and umami. Like most things in your body, taste buds don't work alone – you also need your nose in order to be able to fully taste food. This explains why you can't taste much when your nose is stuffed up.

FAST BITE

You've probably experienced how tough it is to eat something really crunchy, like an apple, when you've got a loose tooth, or when you've just lost a tooth. Your teeth are such an important part of your digestive system, so you want to make sure that your permanent teeth are here to stay.

Brush and floss 'em twice a day. If you eat a sticky-sweet or chewy food, like caramel, chewy granola bars, raisins, or even dried fruit strips, you might want to brush when you're finished eating. If your toothbrush is not handy, chewing on cut-up veggies might help get them clean. You might even want to choose snacks like cheese or other protein-rich foods, which are way better for your teeth.

THIS TASTES FAMILIAR, BUT I'VE NEVER HAD IT BEFORE...

Before you were born, you were already figuring out what foods you like and don't like. How is that possible? When you were growing inside your mom (and if you were breastfed as a baby), you were tasting the food she was eating.[4] Scientists have even found that if pregnant rats were fed junk foods instead of their usual rat chow, their babies also preferred to eat higher-calorie foods and ate more of the junk foods and more calories than they needed.

MY MOMMY? NO, UMAMI!

In the early twentieth century, a Japanese scientist named Kikunae Ikeda officially discovered a "fifth taste," which is called umami (you pronounce it ooo-mommy). The umami taste can be described as "savoriness," or "meatiness," and it is the flavor that MSG lends to foods when it is added during the manufacturing or cooking process (for more on MSG, flip back to page 79). Fortunately, there are many ways to get that great umami taste from natural foods like mushrooms, cheese, and meat. YUMami![5]

FAST BITE

Here are some examples of foods that have the tastes that your taste buds can taste!

Salty = salted pretzels
Sour = lemon
Sweet = sugar
Bitter = broccoli rabe (YUM!)
Umami = Parmesan cheese

WHAT'S THAT SMELL?

The smell from food can either make you hungry or it can really gross you out. Some foods are particularly pungent, like certain cheeses, or cauliflower when it's cooking. What makes certain foods so stinky? In foods like Limburger and Munster cheese, friendly bacteria break down proteins and create a distinct smell – a pretty bad one at that! On the other hand, when cauliflower is cooked, certain chemicals inside the vegetable break down and release sulfur, which will give your kitchen a pretty funky odor. While these foods may stink, they taste great![6, 7]

However, there's another reason that a food may stink: it might be that the food is old and is not safe to eat. In this case, the smell comes from bad bugs that live on the food as it gets older. When this happens, your nose protects you from eating these bad bugs that can make you really sick.

It really helps to know about food safety, because there are some really sneaky bacteria that make no smell at all. You'll read more about food safety in Chapter 5.

Quirky Food Effects

Q: Why do I get ice cream headaches?

A: When you eat ice cream very quickly, signals from the top of your mouth get sent to your brain. This causes a slight change in your blood flow, which can give you a headache. Don't worry – these headaches don't last long (10 to 30 seconds) and they are not really bad for you. To avoid these headaches, try eating your ice cream slowly and enjoy the flavor!

Q: Why do I get hiccups?

A: Hiccups can happen when you eat too quickly or when you eat hot or cold foods. Both of these conditions cause the muscle at the bottom of your lungs, called the diaphragm, to go into spasm. If you try to breathe in quickly, that rush of incoming air causes a hiccup. Hiccups usually last for just a few minutes and then they usually go away on their own. What is the longest time that a person has had the hiccups? Sixty years! Yikes![8]

A Note About Choking

When a person chokes, their food accidentally goes down "the wrong pipe": instead of going down the esophagus to the stomach, the food goes into the trachea, which is the tunnel to the lungs. While a person can choke on any food, hot dogs and grapes can be particularly dangerous. This is because they are the perfect size to block the air tube, and because they are soft foods, they can be hard to "pop out" of the airway.

So, to keep yourself safe, be sure to pay more attention when you're eating: chew your food carefully and please don't talk with your mouth full because it increases your risk of choking (and you don't want anything falling out of your mouth either!).

It is also really important to know what to do if you or someone else is choking. Talk to your parent(s) about taking a simple first aid course at your local chapter of the Red Cross, or at your local community center.

2. FROM THE STOMACH TO THE INTESTINES

Once in your stomach, that bite of sandwich gets mixed and churned even more by the strong muscles of your stomach. Acid and enzymes from the stomach help to break down the protein and fat in the cheese into smaller pieces.

At this point, what was once bread and cheese is now a soupy mess. Your stomach is also a holding zone, so once you've chewed and swallowed your whole sandwich, the mashed food can stay in your stomach for a few hours. When the pieces of the sandwich are small enough, they move on to the small intestines.

DID YOU KNOW?

WHAT MAKES YOU THROW UP?

Puking is one way that your body protects itself: if you eat something with bad bacteria, if you eat too much, or if you have a stomach virus, your body basically says, "No, thank you!" Your strong stomach muscles flex and force the food to come right back up.

3. FROM THE SMALL INTESTINE TO THE LARGE INTESTINE

Once your soupy mess of cheese sandwich reaches the small intestine, even more chemicals arrive to break down the food. Enzymes from the pancreas and juices from the liver and from cells of the wall of the intestines completely break down all of the macronutrients into their smallest pieces: most of your carbs are now simple sugars (monosaccharides), the fat has been broken down into fatty acids, and the protein is now smaller amino acids.

At this point, the walls of the intestine absorb the monosaccharides, the fatty acids, the amino acids, and all of the vitamins and minerals from the soupy mess. Once they have passed through the wall of the small intestine, they flow through the bloodstream and make their way to different parts of the body. The liver plays a big role in taking in these macros and making them into energy that the body can use. This part of the digestive process usually takes anywhere from about 3 - 10 hours.[9]

While all of the micronutrients and most of the macronutrients have been broken down and absorbed, the fiber from the whole grain bread can't be digested by your body. So, the fiber and any other stuff that your body cannot use moves in a watery solution through the small intestines and into the large intestines.

Q: IF I SWALLOW A PIECE OF GUM, DOES IT GET STUCK IN MY INTESTINES FOR YEARS?

A: No. Gum is made up of rubbery ingredients from plants, but gum doesn't provide your body with any nutrients. So, your body will get rid of your gum with any undigested food and other "waste" in your poop. So, don't worry – you're gum doesn't STICK around!

WANT TO TAKE A FREE THROW SHOT?

Guess how long your small intestines are? No really, guess. Believe it or not, they are about 15 feet (457 cm) long, which is the same distance from the free throw line on a basketball court to the backboard. Add the length of your large intestines to that (which are about 3 feet – 91 cm – long), and you've got 18 feet (550 cm). While you can do a free throw in a matter of seconds, it can take over 24 hours or more for all of your food to travel through your intestines.

4. THE END: LARGE INTESTINE

Once all of the stuff that your body doesn't need flows into the large intestine, some water is absorbed into the colon, making the leftovers less liquid. The leftovers make their way thorough the colon and then on to the last part of the large intestine, the rectum. The waste, which is now officially poop, then comes out of your anus.

Most kids have about one or two poops a day, while some only have one every other day (this means leftovers stay in your colon for a pretty long time!). It all depends on the amount of fiber that someone eats, how much liquid they drink, and what kinds of fruits and vegetables they eat. More than one half of the weight of poop is water, and the rest is stuff from your food that your body doesn't need, cells from the lining of the intestines, and even dead bugs!

KEEP YOUR BOWELS MOVING

One of the main reasons kids get stomachaches is constipation.[10] Constipation happens when your poops move too slowly through your intestines, and your intestine absorbs too much of the water in your poops. This makes them dry, hard, and very painful to pass. Also, gases build up and get trapped behind the poops, which can cause you a lot of pain and bloating.

So, how can you keep your intestines in tip-top form? Fluids and fiber. Water keeps your poops soft, so be sure you drink enough water every day (flip back to page 88 to see how much water you need). Fiber ensures that your poops moves through your intestines at a regular pace. You can make really simple changes in your diet to make sure that you get enough fiber (most kids do not get enough).[11] The following foods give you about 30 grams of fiber, which, when eaten over the span of one day, will give you all of the fiber you need in a day.

- 2 slices whole grain bread
- 1 pear
- 1 apple
- 1/2 cup (125 mL) dried apricots
- 1/2 cup (125 mL) blueberries
- 1 cup (250 mL) whole grain pasta
- 1/2 cup (125 mL) chickpeas (these can be added to pastas and salads, if not on their own, or mashed to make a nice dip – see Chapter 4 for an avocado and chickpea hummus recipe).
- 1/2 cup (125 mL) peas

Q: UM, WHAT EXACTLY ARE BUGS DOING IN MY BODY?

A: There are about 100 trillion good bugs that live in your small and large intestines. Taken altogether, they probably weigh about three pounds (1.4 kilograms)! These microscopic rice-shaped bugs are called the gut flora and they do a lot to keep you healthy: they make some vitamin K and they fight off bad bugs that can get in through your food.

(Continued on the next page.)

(Continued from the previous page.)

They also make your poops and your farts stink, because when the bugs break down certain parts of your food, they create a very smelly gas. Scientists are still figuring out all of the different roles that these gut bugs play.

While these bugs are obviously really powerful, sometimes they need a little help to get the job done. Probiotics are healthy bugs that are found in some foods, like yogurt. Probiotics are similar to the other healthy bugs already in your intestines, so when you eat them, they get along well. If you've taken antibiotic medicine for an infection, the number of healthy bugs in your intestines can get lower. Probiotics may help to rebuild a strong healthy bug community in there.[12]

So even though some of them stink, you should be thrilled to have these bugs around!

YOUR BREAD IS GASSY!

Most breads are made with an ingredient called yeast. Yeast is actually a living organism and it eats sugar, which is usually an ingredient in bread recipes. When the yeast digests the sugar, it produces gas, just like you do when you digest food. This creates little pockets of air in the bread you eat, making it softer, which you can see in every slice.

Use 'Em Up!

Now that we've talked poops, let's go back and see what happens to those nutrients: they've passed through the wall of your intestines and have been sent all over your body through your bloodstream. Vitamins and minerals enter cells and get to work helping you grow, heal, and move your muscles. Amino acids (from proteins) help to build muscles and many other body structures. So it turns out you really are what you eat!

So that leaves us with monosaccharides from carbs and fatty acids from fats. Your cells use the these for energy (some of the amino acids are also used for energy). This means that your body can grow, or you can walk the dog, do a science experiment, or figure out your math homework.

Usually, you will have some extra monosaccharides and fatty acids left over that your body doesn't need right away. When this happens, your body stores them as fat. These fat reserves are absolutely essential to good health – they are like an "energy warehouse" that your body can tap into when necessary (some of the simple sugars are stored in your liver and muscles for quick energy boosts too). Also, your body stores fat-soluble vitamins A, D, E, and K in there. Even the fittest athlete needs to have some fat reserves in their body to stay healthy!

But what about *your* fat reserves? Well, if you remain inactive on a regular basis, your body will build up fat reserves to store a lot of the energy from your food. This is what people call "gaining weight," because your fat reserves are actually getting bigger.

If you exercise pretty hard on a regular basis, you will use up the energy from your food, and then your body will tap into your stored body fat for energy. When this happens, people call it "losing weight," because you are literally using up your body's fat reserves.

So how can you find the balance that works for you, so that you have a right amount of fat in your body? Combine good nutrition with regular exercise!

Work it On Out

Your body needs to move in order to stay healthy. There are so many different exercises to choose from (check out our "Tools" section at the back of the book for a variety of exercises). Just remember that no matter what activity or sport you choose, you need to be moving a lot for one whole hour in order to give your body a good workout.

Keeping your body fat balanced is a really important benefit of regular "cardio" exercise. However, that's not the only reason you should exercise. It turns out that when you exercise:

→ Your body releases endorphins, which are chemicals that make you feel really happy.

→ You will sleep better.

→ You will be better able to handle stress.

→ You will feel good about yourself. [13, 14]

Q: What exactly is "cardio" exercise?

A: It is any kind of exercise that keeps your heart pumping and gets your body to tap into its fat stores for energy. It also makes your heart muscles stronger and your lungs healthier. It is the most useful kind of exercise in terms of keeping your body balanced.

Q: How do I know if I am exercising in a "cardio" range?

A: You could count the number of times your heart beats in a minute and compare it to a chart, but that will probably interrupt the activity you're doing. A really easy way to tell if you are in the cardio range is to see if you are breathing heavily but can still carry on a conversation with someone. If you are huffing and puffing and you can't get a word out, slow down. If your breathing is still really easy, then pick it up!

TRY SOMETHING NEW

When you try a new sport or activity, you develop different skills and different muscles, which ensures that your body doesn't get too comfortable and used to particular movements.

It's no secret that football players in the National Football League have trained in ballet, jazz ballet, and tap to improve their flexibility and agility. Lynn Swann, a former receiver for the Pittsburgh Steelers and a member of the Pro Football Hall of Fame has said, "Certain dance movements are fundamental to the movements you need to make in sports," and that, "A basketball player can't jump without doing a plié. It may not be graceful and deep ... but it's the same thing."[15]

And while physical activities like ballet, yoga, and pilates can increase your flexibility and balance, your body still needs to do activities that encourage strength building and that make your heart rate get into the cardio range. So it's important for you to combine different activities as part of your exercise.

To incorporate two different activities into your schedule, like yoga and soccer, you've got lots of possibilities: play 30 minutes of soccer, then do 30 minutes of yoga per day. Or you could do yoga one day for an hour, then play soccer for an hour the next day. Or, you could even stick with yoga as your activity for six to eight weeks, then switch to soccer. It's up to you!

Did you Know?

Your brain needs energy too, and its main source is carbs. But your brain needs more than just that: more than half of your brain cells are important fat cells. Omega-3 fat that is found in fish, soybeans, and walnuts (YUM!) makes up a large part of these brain cells. That is why fish is often referred to as "brain food." Other healthy fats like olive oil, avocados, and pecans also help build the wall that surrounds the brain. So it's okay to have a FAT head!

Give it a Rest

Your body works around the clock – not only does it digest your food and keep you moving during sports and other activities, it also makes sure that all of your basic body functions are happening. When you sleep, you give your body a bit of a break. During deep sleep, your body repairs damaged tissues, like cuts or pulled muscles. It releases different hormones (our chemical messengers), which have many effects: some of them cause tissue growth and development, while others regulate your appetite. Also, your muscles "shut down" while you sleep so that you can save your energy reserves for your daytime activities.[16]

When you sleep well over many nights, you are better able to pay attention in class and to think creatively and solve problems. However, if you generally don't get enough sleep, you are more likely to be in a bad mood and you are more likely to get sick.[17]

So just how many zzzzzs should you be getting? Kids generally need anywhere from 9 to 12 hours of sleep every night (just like calories, the number of hours of sleep you need is a very individual thing).[18]

So, it's really important that you find a good balance between the energy going into your body from your food, and the energy going out of your body when you exercise, and when you grow. That's how you achieve a balance that's just right for you.

Kids between the ages of 8 and 13 need anywhere from 1,600 to 2,600 calories every day. Obviously, there is a wide range of what is considered a "normal" amount of calories for kids. This is because different kids have different needs: some kids are really active all the time, while others are less active. Also, when your body is going through a big period of growth, you will need more calories than normal. In addition, boys generally need more calories than girls.

Q: AW MAN, DOES THIS MEAN I NEED TO COUNT CALORIES?

A: No, you totally do not have to count calories. While it is generally good to know how many calories you need (and it can be a useful thing for adults to do when they need to lose or gain weight), counting calories is not a useful thing to do when you're young.

The best way to make sure you're getting what you need is to eat a variety of foods in balanced meals and snacks. If you want to count something, count the number of fruits and veggies you eat every day, or the number of new foods you try every week. Make sure those add up!

Balance is the goal when it comes to energy going in and coming out of your body. When your body is in balance, your body is in its healthiest shape and you feel your best.

THE RIGHT AMOUNT OF ENERGY FROM A VARIETY OF FOODS + THE RIGHT AMOUNT OF PHYSICAL ACTIVITY = HEALTHY AMOUNT OF BODY FAT

If this is where you are right now, here are some tips to keep you balanced:

⊖ Eat a little bit of all foods (see Chapter 4 for tasty recipes that will keep your taste buds on their toes).

⊖ Pick foods that have whole grains and polyunsaturated fats.

⊖ Choose fruits and vegetables as snacks, and have them with yogurt dip or other dip, if desired.

⊖ Include foods that have protein and iron in each meal.

⊖Read food labels to help guide your food choices.

⊖Stay active – do about one hour of some type of exercise or activity every day.

⊖ Be aware of your thirst and hunger cues – remember that they are different!

Q: HOW CAN I BE SURE OF HOW MUCH BODY FAT IS RIGHT FOR ME?

A: The next time you have a checkup with your doctor, ask him or her how much body fat is right for you. Your doctor will be able to give you an answer based on your weight, your height, and something called your **Body Mass Index**. They will be able to let you know whether or not you should be making some changes to your activity level and/or to how you are eating.

Sometimes, you will make choices about food or exercise that aren't so great – everyone does, but there is no reason to freak out. However, you need to know that when you make choices like these often over a long period of time, your body can get out of balance.

TOO MUCH ENERGY FROM FOOD + LIMITED PHYSICAL ACTIVITY = EXTRA BODY FAT

There are many reasons why kids consume too much energy: some regularly eat high-calorie foods, like chips, donuts, and chocolate bars; some regularly eat servings that are too large; some regularly skip breakfast, which might actually make them eat more than they need later; and some kids often ignore the signals they get from their brains telling them they're full or that they are actually thirsty, not hungry.

There are also plenty of reasons why kids don't get enough exercise: some are busy doing low-energy activities, like playing video games, surfing the Internet, or watching TV or a movie. Time flies during these activities, and can add up to 3 - 4 hours a day! Also, many schools have cut back on the amount of time that kids spend in gym class.

DID YOU KNOW?

MIXED MESSAGES

Foods that are labeled "diet" usually contain additives, like aspartame, which add a sweet flavor but don't add calories. But it has been found that "diet" foods may actually make some overweight kids gain more weight.[19] How does that work? Well, when kids eat diet foods, their brains get mixed signals: while the food tastes sweet, the body does not get any energy from this "fake sugar," so the brain does not get the message that the body is satisfied. So, the brain keeps telling the body, "Eat more! Eat more!" This means that kids may end up eating a large quantity of diet food or that kids eventually choose to eat a non-diet food to stop their cravings.

Be kind to your body and your brain: choose a variety of naturally low-sugar foods for your meals and snacks, and choose diet foods less often (unless you are diabetic).

If you have too much body fat, you can follow all of the tips on keeping balanced on page 104, and you can try these out too:

⊖ Choose lower fat, lower calorie foods more often. But don't limit fats too much. You should keep eating healthy fats (like nuts and seeds, and avocados) that your body needs for growth and health.

⊖ Watch your portions when you're out – ask to take 1/2 of the meal home; eat only 1/2 of a large muffin or bagel and save the rest for later.

⊖ Try to get 100% of your DV of fiber every day.

⊖ Eat fruits and vegetables for snacks – try to stay away from the high-fat and salty snacks, like chips.

⊖ Choose 1 % or 2 % milk instead of 3.25 % or whole milk.

⊖ If you are playing games on the computer every day, change to 3 - 4 times a week, or stay on for 20 - 30 minutes only. Make time to do a sport or an activity.

⊖ Find a sport or an activity that you really like and start doing it three times a week for 30 minutes. Try to slowly work your way up to five days a week.

⊖ Drink water instead of sugary drinks or juices – limit these to only a couple of times a week; dilute juices with at least 1/2 water.

NOT ENOUGH ENERGY FROM FOOD + TOO MUCH PHYSICAL ACTIVITY = NOT ENOUGH BODY FAT

There are plenty of reasons why some kids are not getting enough energy from the food they eat: some kids eat really small serving sizes that do not provide the right amount of nutrients. Some kids skip meals, either by choice or because there is simply not enough food in their homes. Some kids purposely eat very little food to try to stay thin.

While physical activity is awesome, some kids who train regularly for sports burn off a lot of calories, and don't replace those lost calories with healthy snacks or larger meals. This kind of imbalance can seriously interfere with your growth.

GOOD IDEA!

For kids who are having trouble keeping their body fat level within a healthy range, it is a good idea to see a registered dietitian to get advice. There are organizations that can help you find a dietitian in your area: the Dietitians of Canada (www.dietitians.ca) and the American Dietetic Association (www.eatright.org).

If you have too little body fat, you can follow all of the tips on keeping balanced on page 104, and you can try these out too:

→ Add extra calories by choosing foods with healthy fats, like nuts, seeds, and avocados, and add them to salads, rice, and vegetables; make yogurt smoothies with extra cream for added energy.

→ Try your best not to skip meals or snacks.

→ Choose higher fat milk like 3.25 % or whole milk for extra calories.

→ Dip fruits and vegetables in yogurt or another creamy dip.

→ Put an extra slice of cheese in your sandwich, extra butter on your bagel.

→ Stay active, but eat high-energy snacks, like granola, to keep up your energy reserves.

THE "IDEAL" BODY

If you take a look at television, movies, and advertisements, you will see that typically, female celebrities are quite thin, and male celebrities are lean and muscular. While many celebrities have found their own balance of healthy eating and exercise (we've got quotes from some of them in this book!), many other celebrities go to extremes to keep their bodies in a certain shape. Some famous people have even admitted to having eating disorders like anorexia, bulimia, and binge eating.

Right now, your body needs a lot of energy and nutrients to grow and develop properly. This is a time to eat well, enjoy your food, and exercise daily. And while it is awesome, and even helpful, to be inspired by healthy celebrities, it is important to remember that the ideal body is one that is well fueled and healthy, not super-skinny or super-muscular.

WHAT CELEBS SAY

Actress America Ferrera:

"It's not about looking like a supermodel [...] It's about feeling good about who I am."[20]

Actor Zac Efron:

"Working out is my biggest hobby [...] It's my Zen hour. I just zone out."[21]

Actress Jessica Alba:

"I run a little, bike a little, lift some weights [...]. And I still [...] eat dessert. I think everything in moderation is cool."[22]

Feeling good!

What an amazing body – it takes care of you, so you have to take care of it too! Now you know the following:

→ How to recognize your hunger and thirst signals.

→ Digestion is the process that breaks your food down into pieces that your body can use.

→ You need fat reserves to stay healthy.

→ It's important to exercise every day for one hour in the "cardio range."

→ You need to balance your food intake with exercise to ensure that you have a healthy amount of body fat.

Now let's check out how to make great food choices with different meals and snacks that give your body what it needs.

CHAPTER

4

EATING WELL THROUGHOUT THE DAY

MEALS AND SNACKS TO FUEL YOUR DAY!

Eating well is a key part of staying healthy. However, eating well day-to-day is not just about giving your body carbs, fats, proteins, vitamins, and minerals – it is also about feeding your body the right nutrients *throughout* the day. When you consistently eat breakfast, lunch, dinner, and snacks, you provide your body with a steady stream of the nutrients that it really needs.

Eating well also involves getting the right nutrients from a variety of foods. By eating a little bit of this and a little bit of that, you are much more likely to get all of the nutrients you need than if you keep eating the same foods over and over again.

So how do you plan a healthy, delicious meal? Or even a snack? This can seem like a pretty overwhelming thing to do, but this chapter will show you exactly how do it.

So, let's take a look at some irresistible meal and snack ideas that you can use any day of the week.

FIRST THINGS FIRST:

Cooking is fun and is a pretty cool skill to have. More and more kids are taking cooking lessons that are offered at grocery stores or in schools. There are some fantastic recipes in this book, and you might be inspired to go online and find other recipes you want to try. Here are some pointers to help you get through reading and preparing food using a recipe:

1. Let your parent(s) know that you're planning to cook.

2. If your recipe involves sharp kitchen utensils, electric appliances, the stove or the oven, make sure that there's an adult around to help you out.

3. Read all the way through the recipe once to make sure you understand what you need to do.

4. Make sure you have all of the ingredients you need and then set them aside.

5. Next, get out the measuring cups and spoons that you will need.

6. Get your preparation space ready by washing any cutting surfaces and ensuring that all pots, pans, and other kitchen tools are clean.

7. Roll up your sleeves and wash your hands well (check out Chapter 5 for more ideas about food safety in your kitchen).

Now you're cooking!

hile lunch, supper, and snacks are all vital to your day, breakfast really is the most important meal. Why? Well, think about it: after you've slept for about 8-10 hours, the levels of carbs in your blood are probably pretty low. This means that your organs and your brain are ready for more fuel. In fact, the word breakfast actually comes from being ready to "break" your "fast" from overnight. Also, if you miss breakfast, it's really tough to make up for it later on in the day because your body still has to spend the whole morning lagging behind. So bring on the breakfast!

FAST BITE

There are a lot of kids who don't eat breakfast each morning.[1,2] Because breakfast is so important to kids' growth and development, many schools have breakfast programs where adults serve healthy food to kids before classes start. If your school has a breakfast program and you're not already part of it, consider helping out: you can help the adults serve food, or you can see if it's possible to sit with some of the younger kids and keep them company while they eat.

Did You Know?

By having a good breakfast, believe it or not, you are more likely to:

• be able to solve math problems better, remember things you learned more clearly, and get better grades;
• be more energetic;
• have a healthy level of body fat. [3, 4]

Good Idea!

BECOME AN EARLY RISER

Too rushed in the morning to eat breakfast? Think about getting up 15 minutes earlier. Even a few extra minutes will make a big difference in whether or not you eat, and what you eat in the morning. Another idea: with the help of your parent(s), prepare French toast or bacon and eggs the night before so all you have to do is heat it up in the morning.

HERE ARE SEVEN NUTRIENT-RICH SUGGESTIONS FOR A NUTRITIOUS AND DELICIOUS BREAKFAST:

⊕ 2 pancakes (see recipe on page 122) + 2 Tbsp (25 mL) vanilla yogurt with 1 Tbsp (15 mL) seeds + 1 cup (250 mL) milk + fresh orange

⊕ 1-2 cups (250 - 500 mL) yogurt smoothie (see recipe on page 120) + 1/2 whole grain English muffin with nut butter

⊕ 1 cup (250 mL) oatmeal (see page 121) + 1 cup (250 mL) milk + 1/2 banana

⊕ 1-2 scrambled or boiled eggs (tip: make an extra boiled egg and have it for lunch the next day) + whole wheat bagel with butter + 1 cup (250 mL) milk + pear slices

⊕ Breakfast cereal (whole grain variety) + milk for cereal + 1/2 cup fresh or frozen berries

⊕ 2 slices whole wheat toast + nut butter + 1 cup (250 mL) milk + 2 kiwi fruit, sliced

⊕ Chicken leg from night before (YUM!) or 1 cup (250 mL) lentil salad + 1/2 whole wheat bagel + 1 cup (250 mL) milk + 4 slices melon

WHAT CELEBS SAY

Actress Heather Locklear, on her daughter Ava's eating habits:

"Ava's a great eater. She only eats things like fruits and vegetables and sushi — no junk food ... It's ironic because I want to set a good example for her with my eating habits, and she's the one who's helping me!"[5]

Did You Know?

... that kids around the world eat many different things for breakfast? In the Netherlands, along with different foods that include breads, meats, cheeses, and yogurt, kids might be sliding some green pickled herrings into their mouths. In Bulgaria, they might be starting their day with cheese, honey, olives, tomatoes, and yogurt. In Greece, children might be offered yogurt and fresh fruit, cheese, and some honey. In Vietnam, kids might start their day with sticky rice with nuts or some spicy soups. In Egypt, kids might have beans or lentils cooked in lemon juice, olive oil, and garlic, while in Ethiopia breakfast may be flatbread or some kind of porridge or stew. Now that's variety!

FROSTED CHOCOLATE MARSHMALLOW CEREALS: AN UNHEALTHY WAY TO START YOUR DAY

Are you a die-hard cereal eater at breakfast time? Most people have a few favorite cereals that they have for breakfast. Unfortunately, many of these cereals are loaded with sugar and salt (yup, you read that right – be sure to read those labels!). They are usually pretty weak sources of fiber too.

Do you need to give up your fave cereal? No way. What you can do is try mixing 1/2 of a serving of your usual cereal with 1/2 of a serving of a whole grain cereal. This is a great way to get more fiber, vitamins, minerals, and longer-lasting energy and still have the taste of your old favorite.

Also, if you have cereal every day, try cutting cereal down to two breakfasts per week, and try different foods, such as eggs, smoothies, and yogurt.

WHAT CELEBS SAY

Actress Denise Richards:
"Eating small meals with a balance of protein and fiber keeps me going.... I always have breakfast. Lately it's scrambled eggs, pancakes, toast, or whatever I've made for the kids at 7 a.m."[10]

GIVE IT A TRY!

SCRUMPTIOUS SMOOTHIE

Place the following ingredients in a blender and blend until smooth:

1 cup (250 mL) plain or vanilla yogurt
1 cup (250 mL) milk
1 very ripe pear, chopped into smaller pieces
1 whole ripe banana, sliced
1/2 cup (125 mL) berries (frozen or fresh)
4 Tbsp (50 mL) ground flaxseeds

Makes about 4 cups (1 L). Any leftovers can be kept in the refrigerator and used later as a great after-school or pre-sports snack.

One serving (1 cup or 250 mL) provides:
168 calories; 6 grams fat (9 % DV); 2.0 grams saturated fat (10 % DV); 10.5 mg cholesterol (3 % DV); 69 mg sodium (3 % DV); 6.5 grams protein; 24.5 grams carbohydrate (8 % DV); 4.6 grams fiber (18 % DV); 1 mg iron (7 % DV); 188 mg calcium (17 % DV); 231 IU vitamin A (7% DV); 5 mg vitamin C (8 % DV)

WHAT CELEBS SAY

NHL player Jarome Iginla:

"[One thing I can't live without is] my blender: I use it to make healthy drinks, smoothies."[7]

GIVE IT A TRY!

THE BEST-EVER OATMEAL

- 1/2 cup (125 mL) cooked oats – preferably steel-cut oats (available at most large chain grocery stores)
- 1/2 sliced banana, pear, peach, or 1/2 cup (125 mL) fresh berries (or mix these up!)
- 4 Tbsp (50 mL) plain or vanilla yogurt
- 1 Tbsp (15 mL) maple syrup (only if you're using plain yogurt)
- 1 Tbsp (15 mL) walnuts
- 1 Tbsp (15 mL) sesame seeds

Tip: Put this together the night before, layering oats with yogurt, fruit, and nuts, and it will be ready to eat in the morning. You can even make a couple at the same time and have one as a pre-sports or after-school snack.

Makes 1 serving.

One serving (1 cup or 250 mL) provides:
394 calories; 14 grams fat (22 % DV); 2.5 grams saturated fat (12 %); 8 mg cholesterol (3 % DV); 9.8 mg sodium (< 1 % DV); 10 grams protein; 60.2 grams carbohydrate (20 % DV); 7.3 grams fiber (30 % DV); 3.4 mg iron (24 % DV); 206 mg calcium (19 % DV); 100 IU vitamin A (3% DV); 5 mg vitamin C (8 % DV)

HOW REAL KIDS EAT RIGHT

LIAM TEITELBAUM, AGE 8

Why I eat healthy foods: So I can grow.

My favorite healthy snacks:
- Cream cheese
- Peanut butter & jelly sandwich
- Bananas
- Watermelon
- Yogurt

My favorite recipe: Waffles – flour, eggs, baking powder, water, oil, vanilla.

My tip for healthy eating: Eat fruit!

GIVE IT A TRY!

PANCAKES WITH A PUNCH

Mix the dry ingredients together and store in the cupboard, then add the liquid part when you are ready to eat:

1 1/2 cups (375 mL) whole wheat flour
3/4 cup (175 mL) rolled oats
2 Tbsp (25 mL) brown sugar
4 Tbsp (50 mL) wheat germ
4 Tbsp (50 mL) ground flaxseeds
1 tsp (5 mL) baking powder
1/4 tsp (1 mL) salt

For every 1 1/4 cup (300 mL) of dry ingredients (or about one half of the recipe of dry ingredients), add 1 egg, 1 cup (250 mL) milk, 1 tsp (5 mL) lemon juice, 2 Tbsp (25 mL) vegetable or olive oil.
(For a very berry boost, add about 1/2 cup (125 mL) of fresh or frozen blueberries or raspberries to the batter).

Add 2 Tbsp (25 mL) oil to large frying pan, and spoon about 2 Tbsp (25 mL) of batter for each pancake onto pan, heating about 2 minutes on each side over medium heat, until golden brown.

Top with delicious yogurt mixture. Mix together 1/2 cup (125 mL) plain yogurt, 1 mashed banana, and about 2 Tbsp (25 mL) of maple syrup. Sprinkle with walnuts and sesame seeds for added fiber, healthy fats, protein, and calcium. So unbelievably delicious!

Tip: Start with 3/4 cup (175 mL) regular flour and 3/4 cup (175 mL) whole wheat flour. The next time you make the recipe, replace the regular flour with whole wheat flour to help you get used to the different, slightly heavier texture of the whole wheat flour.

Makes 8 servings.

One serving (one pancake) provides:
149 calories; 8.8 grams fat (14 % DV); 1 gram saturated fat (5 %DV); 28 mg cholesterol (9 % DV); 85 mg sodium (4 % DV); 4.5 grams protein; 15 grams carbohydrate (5 % DV); 1.4 grams fiber (6 % DV); 1.1 mg iron (8 % DV); 66 mg calcium (6 % DV); 96 IU vitamin A (3% DV); 0 mg vitamin C (0 % DV); 14 IU vitamin D (7%DV)

My Stomach's Grumbling I need a snack!

Once the recess bell rings, it's a good idea to have a snack – a little pick-me-up that will get your energy revving again. The best snacks have a variety of ingredients and are easy to prepare and easy to eat.

Here are seven snack suggestions:

- 1 sliced apple + 4 whole grain crackers + water
- 1 sliced pear + 1/2 bagel + water
- 1 cranberry walnut muffin (see recipe on page 125) + 1/2 - 1 cup (125 – 250 mL) milk + water
- 8 whole grain crackers + 2 oz (60 g) cheese + water
- 1 cup (250 mL) celery sticks/sliced cucumber + 4 Tbsp (50 mL) avocado hummus or other hummus for veggie dipping (see page 129) + water
- 2 homemade chocolate chip cookies (see recipe on page 138) + 1 cup (250 mL) milk + 1/2 cup berries
- 1/2 large slice pizza (from night before) + 1 cup (250 mL) water + 1/2 sliced apple

What Celebs Say

Actress Vanessa Hudgens:

"[My favorite snack is] peanut butter crackers. I eat them all the time, so I always smell like peanut butter!"[8]

Good Idea!

Energy bars do provide some good nutrients for a quick snack – but it is also easy to make your own energy-rich snack, and without the added sugar and salt that is found in manufactured bars. A homemade jumble of nuts, dried fruits, and crackers is a great alternative!

Get a large container with a seal-tight lid and pack it with some super-energy, super-tasting snacks. For example: combine all sorts of nuts – almonds, cashews, pine nuts, pecans, peanuts; with some seeds, including pumpkin, sunflower, and sesame seeds. Then throw in some raisins, dried apricots, and cranberries. And if you're feeling really saucy, add in some whole grain cereal squares or some rice crackers or whole grain crackers.

You can then pack your "jumble" into a small container for a snack or mini meal on the run, or you can add a sprinkle of it to salads, rice, or pasta dishes, oatmeal, or yogurts.

Buying in Bulk

It's a good idea to buy certain foods in bulk, like nuts, seeds, and dried fruits. When you buy in bulk, you scoop up exactly the quantity of food that you want and you put it into a plastic bag. You bring your plastic bag to the cash register and you pay according to the weight of your bag. There is much less packaging involved when you buy foods in bulk, and buying food this way is usually less expensive than buying pre-packaged food. Just be sure that once you get home, you store that food properly in air-tight containers so that it lasts as long as possible.

Nuts!

About 1 in 100 kids has an allergy to peanuts.[9] This means that you might know someone with this kind of allergy (or you might have the allergy yourself). If you do have this allergy, you already know to avoid peanuts – that's obvious. The peanut is a legume, so that makes it different from other nuts like cashews and almonds, but about one out of every five kids with an allergy to peanuts will have an allergy to other nuts as well.[10] This is why a nut-free rule at school usually applies to all kinds of nuts, including peanuts.

If you don't have this allergy, you need to make sure that if you are baking something that has any kind of nuts as an ingredient that you do not bring it to school (most schools are nut-free anyway) or anywhere there might be someone who you know has a peanut and/or nut allergy. You also have to make sure that if a friend with this allergy comes over to your house, you and your family put away any foods that contain any kind of nuts or traces of nuts. For people with a peanut and/or nut allergy, this is very serious as it's a matter of life or death.

CRANBERRY AND WALNUT MUFFINS

These taste great and have an added crunch from the nuts – but remember, if you have a peanut or nut allergy, don't add the walnuts! And if you make these, don't have them near anyone with a nut allergy.

In a food processor, chop:
1/3 cup (75 mL) dried cranberries and 1/3 cup (75 mL) sugar

In a small bowl, add:
4 Tbsp (50 mL) orange juice to the cranberries and sugar and leave it for a few minutes while you prepare the next ingredients.

In a small pan, lightly toast:
1/2 cup (125 mL) walnuts – heat them up until you smell the walnuts in the air a little bit. Set them aside to cool.

In a bowl, mix together:
1 cup (250 mL) whole wheat flour, 1 tsp (5 mL) baking powder, 1/2 tsp (2 mL) baking soda, and 1/2 tsp (2 mL) salt. Set this aside.

Now, in a different bowl, mix together:
2 eggs, 2 Tbsp (25 mL) sugar, 3 Tbsp (45 mL) butter (softened), 3/4 cup (175 mL) milk, and 1 tsp (5 mL) lemon juice.

Combine the flour and egg mixture into one bowl, and add the cranberries and walnuts. Stir just until the dry ingredients disappear into the wet ingredients – if you mix it too much, your muffins will be rock-hard!

Place in muffin tin that has been lightly greased with oil. Bake at 375° F (190° C) for about 20 minutes.

Make your own version: You don't have to stick with only cranberries and walnuts. You can replace the cranberries with apricots, or raisins, and the walnuts with pecans, or sunflower seeds, for a change.

One serving (1 muffin) provides:
154 calories; 7.2 grams fat (11 % DV); 2.1 grams saturated fat (11 % DV); 44 mg cholesterol (15 % DV); 220 mg sodium (9 % DV); 3.6 grams protein; 19.5 grams carbohydrate (6.5 % DV); 0.8 grams fiber (3 % DV); 0.8 mg iron (6 % DV); 47 mg calcium (4 % DV); 169 IU vitamin A (5 % DV); 2 mg vitamin C (3 % DV)

Fluffy muffins tip: If you have a little more time, separate the egg yellow from the white in 2 different bowls. Beat the egg whites with a mixer until they form small peaks. Add the egg yolks to the butter mixture, and add the egg whites to the batter just before you add the cranberries and walnuts. This will make the muffins a little bit fluffier.

LOVE LUNCH

As with breakfast, many kids feel as if lunch is a meal that is rushed – especially on school days, since eating has to fit into your lunch period among all kinds of other stuff, like playing, hanging out with your friends, and participating in clubs or groups. However, lunch can still be fabulously delicious and good for you.

HERE ARE SEVEN GREAT LUNCH IDEAS:

2 slices whole grain bread + 4 tbsp (50 mL) hummus with avocado (see recipe page 129) (dip bread in hummus) + 1 cup (250 mL) strawberries + 1 cup (250 mL) milk

1-2 (250-500mL) cups bean salad (see recipe on page 130) + 1 slice whole-grain bread + 1 banana +1 cup (250 mL) milk

2 slices whole grain bread + 1-2 cups (250-500 mL) spinach salad + 1 oz (30 g) cheese +1 cup (250 mL) milk

1-2 cups (250-500 mL) cream of broccoli soup with whole wheat pasta added + whole grain bagel + 1 cup (250 mL) milk + 4 melon slices

1-2 cups (250 – 500 mL) pasta with meat sauce + small lettuce salad with vinaigrette dressing +1 cup (250 mL) milk + pear slices

1/2 - 1 cup (125-250 mL) lentil salad + 1 cup sliced cucumbers and carrots + 2 Tbsp (25 mL) creamy dip for vegetables + 1 cup (250 mL) milk + 1 slice whole grain bread + 1 cup (250 mL) strawberries

1 -2 cups (250- 500 mL) quinoa salad mixed with sweet peas + 1 cup (250 mL) cherry tomatoes + 1 cup (250 mL) milk + 1 cup (250 mL) blueberries

GIVE IT A TRY!

JAZZED-UP HUMMUS

Mix together:
- 1 cup (250 mL) canned chickpeas, drained
- 1 ripe avocado (remove the skin, cut away the fleshy part, slice, and discard the pit)
- 4 Tbsp (50 mL) your very favorite salsa

One serving (4 Tbsp or 60 mL) provides:
78 calories; 4 grams fat (6 % DV); 0.5 grams saturated fat (3 % DV); 0 mg cholesterol (0 % DV); 140 mg sodium (6 % DV); 2.1 grams protein; 9.4 grams carbohydrate (3 % DV); 3.1 grams fiber (12 % DV); 0.6 mg iron (4 % DV); 15 mg calcium (1 % DV); 67 IU vitamin A (2 % DV); 4 mg vitamin C (6 % DV)

SPREADS FROM AROUND THE WORLD

Using a spread like hummus on whole grain bread or crackers is a wonderful way to get a kick of nutrients and flavor in your diet. Here are some other spreads from all over the globe that you might also want to try (you can find some in your local supermarket, or you can find recipes for them online):

Baba Ghanouj: A Middle Eastern spread made with eggplant.
Guacamole: A smooth Latin American spread made with avocados, tomatoes and spices.
Tapenade: A spread from France that is made with mashed olives and garlic.
Taramosalata: A yummy Greek spread made with fish eggs, lemon juice, and onions.

DID YOU KNOW?

In ancient Greece, many people did not use cloth napkins (or paper napkins!) to clean their hands during a meal. Instead, they wiped their hands on pieces of bread.[11]

GIVE IT A TRY!

BEAN-A-LICIOUS SALAD

In a large bowl, combine:
- 1 clove of garlic, crushed
- 8 fl. oz (270 mL) each of canned chickpeas and red kidney beans, both drained and rinsed
- 3/4 cup (175 mL) fresh green beans, cut into pieces
- 6 fl. oz (180 mL) canned whole kernel corn, undrained
- 1/4 small red onion, diced

In a separate bowl, mix together:
- 3 Tbsp (45 mL) olive oil
- 2 Tbsp (25 mL) dried basil
- 4 tsp (20 mL) sugar
- 4 tsp (20 mL) balsamic vinegar
- 1/2 tsp (2 mL) salt
- 1/2 tsp (2 mL) black pepper

Add this dressing to bean mixture and stir to coat. Take 1 cup of the salad in a container along with some whole grain pita bread for lunch. YUM!

Tips:
- To decrease the salt content, use dried chickpeas and red kidney beans, and boil them as directed on the package.
- To mix it up, try adding some favorite whole grain pasta or brown rice to the bean salad. These can be used instead of pita bread as your source of carbs with this salad.

Makes 4 servings.

One serving (1 cup or 250 mL) provides:
284 calories; 11.2 grams fat (17 % DV); 0 grams saturated fat (0 % DV); 0 mg cholesterol (0 % DV); 758 mg sodium (32 % DV); 7.9 grams protein; 39 grams carbohydrate (13 % DV); 8.7 grams fiber (35 % DV); 3 mg iron (21 % DV); 74 mg calcium (7 % DV); 191 IU vitamin A (6 % DV); 7.3 mg vitamin C (12 % DV)

ON THE RUN AFTER SCHOOL?

ACTIVATE YOUR BODY WITH HEALTHY MINI MEALS.

Organized sports such as soccer, hockey, and swimming are such a big part of life these days. Playing these sports is a great way to stay active and in good health. However, these activities often take place after school and may involve some traveling time to get to the arena, gym, or pool where they take place. So, you may have very little time to sit down to eat a healthy supper before your activity starts. Does this mean that you should go into the big game on an empty stomach? Nope – all you need to do is grab a super-power mini meal.

HERE ARE SEVEN SUGGESTIONS FOR MINI MEALS:

→ 1-2 cups (250-500 mL) yogurt smoothie + 1/2 whole wheat bagel + water

→ 1 cup (250 mL) quinoa (or wheat berries or a combination of the two!) with added feta, peas, seeds, mushrooms + water + orange slices

→ whole wheat wrap with 1/2-1 oz (15-30 g) cheese and 1/2 cup (125 mL) cut-up chicken + 1/2 cup (125 mL) carrot sticks + water + sliced pears

→ 1/2 cup (125 mL) hummus + 1-2 slices whole grain bread or 1 large whole grain pita bread + water + sliced apple

→ 1/2 turkey or egg sandwich (1 slice lean turkey or 1 hard boiled egg mashed on whole wheat bread) with 2-3 slices avocado and 1 lettuce leaf + 1 cup (250 mL) chocolate milk + 1 cup (250 mL) melon cubes

→ 1-2 cups (250-500 mL) asparagus soup with added quinoa + water

→ 1 cup (250 mL) mixed nuts / seeds / dried fruit combination + cucumber slices + water

WHAT CELEBS SAY

Olympic gold medalist Mia Hamm:

"We ate very healthy meals growing up and were always active — at the pool or playing games with my friends .... Fresh, healthy food is only part of the equation .... Living fresh requires getting active and changing the way we think about food, exercise, and our overall health and wellness."[12]

SUPER SUPPER

You're at the end of the day and you're ready for a hearty meal.

CHECK OUT THESE SEVEN SUGGESTIONS FOR A HEALTHY, BALANCED SUPPER:

→ 2-3 chicken thighs (see recipe on page 136) + 1/2 cup (125 mL) peas mixed with 1/2 cup (125 mL) millet (a healthy grain) + 1/2 cup (125 mL) salad with olive oil/balsamic vinegar dressing + 1 cup (250 mL) milk + 2 kiwifruit

→ 1-2 lentil patties (see recipe on page 135) + 1/2 cup (125 mL) brown rice + 1/2 cup (125 mL) green beans + 1 cup (250 mL) milk + 4 slices of papaya + 1/2 cup (125 mL) ice cream

→ 1/2 cup (125 mL) glazed tofu (see recipe on page 40) + 1 cup (250 mL) brown rice or whole grain pasta + 1/2 cup (125 mL) asparagus + 1/2 cup (125 mL) sliced cucumbers/carrots + 1 cup (250 mL) milk + 4 slices cantaloupe + water

→ grilled salmon + 1/2 cup (125 mL) mango salsa + 1/2-1 cup (125- 250 mL) spelt (a healthy grain) + 1 cup (250 mL) broccoli or cauliflower + 1 cup (250 mL) milk

→ 1-2 cups (250-500 mL) whole wheat pasta with meat sauce + 1 cup (250 mL) green beans + 1 cup (250 mL) milk + 1/2 cup (125 mL) sherbet with 2-4 Tbsp (25 – 50 mL) berries

→ 2-4 beef tacos with melted cheese, salsa, sour cream, chopped carrots, chopped tomatoes + 1 cup (250 mL) milk + 4 slices papaya + water

→ 1 cup sliced chicken breast and cheese (melted) in whole grain tortilla + 1-2 cups (250 -500 mL) spinach and lettuce salad with 2 Tbsp (25 mL) added pine nuts or sesame seeds + vinaigrette + 1 cup (250 mL) whole milk + 1 chocolate cupcake with icing

Eating Like a Snail

Have you ever noticed how rushed life can be? You run around from school to after-school activities, and then home to do your homework, and you barely get any time to actually enjoy the food you eat. Well, in 1986, a group of people in Italy decided that they weren't going to take it anymore and they started the Slow Food movement. People in the Slow Food movement focus on having slow, leisurely meals made with local, fresh ingredients. They also believe that eating with friends and family is absolutely vital to enjoying their food. Give slow eating a try – you might find that you like eating at a snail's pace!

GIVE IT A TRY!

LENTIL BURGERS

Rinse 1 cup (250 mL) dry red lentils and transfer to a saucepan. Add 3 cups (750 mL) water and bring to a boil. Cook for about 30 minutes or until soft. Drain and set aside.

Heat 2 tsp (10 mL) olive oil in a skillet over medium-high heat. Add 2 small onions and 2 large tomatoes, chopped, and 1 small apple that is peeled and chopped. Cook for about 10 minutes until soft.

Transfer apple mixture to the saucepan containing the lentils and add 1/4 cup (50 mL) of bread crumbs. Add 1 tsp (5 mL) sage, a pinch each of black pepper and salt. Then add 1 egg and mix well. Form lentil burgers with your hands.

Roll each patty in a bowl containing 2 cups (500 mL) of bread crumbs to coat the outside of the patties.

In a skillet, add 1 Tbsp (15 mL) olive oil. Heat oil over medium high heat. Place burgers in skillet and cook until crisp. Very carefully add more oil as you need it (up to 3 Tbsp – 45 ml – more).

Makes about 14 patties. Freeze what you won't use immediately in air-tight containers for up to 8 weeks. YUM!

One serving (1 burger or patty) provides:
175 calories; 6 grams fat (9 % DV); 0.7 grams saturated fat (4 % DV); 0 mg cholesterol (0 % DV); 140 mg sodium (6 % DV); 7 grams protein; 24 grams carbohydrate (8 % DV); 5.6 grams fiber (22 % DV); 2.1 mg iron (15 % DV); 47 mg calcium (4 % DV); 243 IU vitamin A (7 % DV); 5 mg vitamin C (8 % DV)

GIVE IT A TRY!

HERBED CHICKEN THIGHS

Preheat your oven to 385° F (190° C).

In a small bowl, combine 3 Tbsp (45 mL) mayonnaise or plain yogurt, 2 Tbsp (25 mL) Dijon mustard, 1 Tbsp (15 mL) lemon juice, 1 tsp (5 ml) each of dried rosemary, dried basil, dried thyme, dried savory, and 2 tsp (10 mL) grated parmesan cheese.

In another medium bowl, mix 2 cups (500 mL) of crushed cornflakes or bran flakes with 1/4 tsp (1 mL) black pepper.

Take 8 boneless, skinless chicken thighs and dip each thigh into the mayonnaise mixture and then in the cereal mixture, making sure they are coated well.

Place the thighs in a baking dish and bake for 35-40 minutes or until juices run clear when you pierce the thighs with a fork. YUM!

One serving (1 chicken thigh) provides:
119 calories; 3 grams fat (5 % DV); 0.8 grams saturated fat (4 %DV); 58 mg cholesterol (19 % DV); 158 mg sodium (6 % DV); 14.7 grams protein; 7.4 grams carbohydrate (2 % DV); 1.4 grams fiber (5 % DV); 3.1 mg iron (22 % DV); 36 mg calcium (3 % DV); 183 IU vitamin A (6 % DV); 0.5 mg vitamin C (< 1 % DV)

HERB IT UP!

One of the easiest ways to add flavor to your meals is to sprinkle on some fresh or dried herbs. Herbs are the tasty edible leaves from certain plants. While it is a lot of fun to experiment with different food and herb combinations, here are a few tried-and-true combos you might want to try:

Tomato sauce, meatballs, and pasta: Oregano and basil
Roasted potatoes: Thyme and rosemary
Burritos: Cilantro (also called coriander)
Fish: Dill or tarragon

Remember that if you are using dried herbs, you will only need a little bit of the herb to give your meal a lot of flavor (start with 1/2 tsp – 2 mL – and keep adding until you like the taste). If you are using fresh herbs, you will need to use more of the herb to season your meal (start with 1 Tbsp – 15 mL – and keep adding until you like the taste).

DELICIOUS DESSERTS

Say it loud, say it proud: desserts are AWESOME! While many people might think that desserts don't belong in your healthy lifestyle, we beg to differ – you just need to make good choices.

Homemade desserts are always better for you than store-bought stuff because you or an adult can control exactly how much sugar, oil, butter, and salt are used. Also, homemade desserts don't have any chemicals added to them to keep them fresh on a shelf in a store. And besides – baking is such a fun thing to do with an adult, like your mom, your dad, your grandpa, or your uncle Bill!

GIVE IT A TRY!

THE BEST-EVER
CHOCOLATE CHIP COOKIES

Mix together 1 cup (250 mL) all-purpose flour, 1 cup (250 mL) rolled oats, 1/4 tsp (1 mL) salt, 1/2 tsp (2 mL) baking powder, and 1/2 tsp (2 mL) baking soda in one bowl.

In another smaller bowl, mix together 1/2 cup (125 mL) butter, softened, 1 cup brown sugar, 1 egg, and 1/2 tsp (2 mL) vanilla extract.

Mix the butter mixture and the flour mixture together. Add 1 1/2 cups (375 mL) semi-sweet chocolate chips to this batter.

Spoon onto greased baking sheet about 1 Tbsp (15 mL) of batter per cookie. Bake at 375° F (190° C) for about 12 minutes, or until they are lightly brown – not too dark or they won't be nice and chewy!

Tip: You can also add walnuts, about 1/2 cup (125 mL) with the chocolate chips if you like for added protein and fiber. YUM!

This recipe makes about 30 cookies. (If you want, you can freeze them in an air-tight container so that you can enjoy them another time.)

One serving (1 cookie) provides:
141 calories; 6.4 grams fat (10 % DV); 3.8 grams saturated fat (19 % DV); 15.5 mg cholesterol (5 % DV); 71 mg sodium (3 % DV); 1.5 grams protein; 19.6 grams carbohydrate (6 % DV); 1.1 grams fiber (4 % DV); 0.7 mg iron (5 % DV); 16 mg calcium (1 % DV); 111 IU vitamin A (3% DV); 0 mg vitamin C (0 % DV)

Rocking Out with Food

There have been many music bands that have included a food item in their names:

Black Eyed Peas , Bread, Cake, The Cranberries, Cream, Meatloaf, Phish, Red Hot Chili Peppers, Salt-n-Pepa, The Sugarcubes, Vanilla Ice, and Vanilla Fudge.

There's even Bananarama, Blind Melon, The Lemonheads, The Meat Puppets, Pearl Jam, and Smashing Pumpkins! Can you think of any others?

Q: OKAY, SO WHAT IF MOM / DAD / GRANDPA / UNCLE BILL HELPS ME COOK A MEAL THAT HAS NEW FOODS IN IT, AND I HATE THE MEAL? HOW DO I TELL THEM THAT I DON'T LIKE IT?

A: This can be a tricky situation. First, remember that it is so nice that Mom / Dad / Grandpa / Uncle Bill worked with you to try something new. This is an adult who loves you, and who supports you as you make a healthy choice.

Now, because this person is so fabulous, you don't want to hurt his or her feelings by saying something like, "This tastes like my old sneakers!" Try saying something like this: "Mom / Dad / Grandpa / Uncle Bill, thanks for helping me make this meal so that I could try something new. The thing is, I don't really like the flavor of it, so I don't think we should make this again. But maybe we could try another recipe soon."

How Real Kids Eat Right

Aidin Abramowitz, age 7

Why I eat healthy foods:
I want to grow, and I don't want to get diabetes like my dad.

My favorite healthy snacks:
- Mandarin oranges
- Applesauce
- Energy bars
- Fruit chewies
- Cookies

My tip for healthy eating:
Try your hardest to eat good foods. You will have more energy and will do better in sports and in school with healthier foods inside you.

Madison Menyuk, age 10

Why I eat healthy foods:
To be strong and healthy.

My favorite healthy snacks:
- Banana
- Apple
- Grapes
- Salad
- Avocados

Nikole Shaham, age 10

Why I eat healthy foods:
Because it means a healthy body, which leads to a long life.

My favorite healthy snacks:
- Nectarine
- Lettuce salad
- Fig bar
- Yogurt
- Wheat crackers

My tip for healthy eating:
Write down what you eat and at the end of the week, see if you need to try to eat better, or if you have been doing well. Also, be sure to try new foods.

You've Got It!

After reading about great food choices and seeing what variety means, along with getting new recipes to try, you are now loaded with lots of ideas to keep your brain and body energized. You now know that:

→ You need to feed your body a steady stream of nutrients from a variety of foods throughout the day.

→ Breakfast truly is the most important meal of the day (do your best to eat it!).

→ Snacks and mini meals are great ways to keep your energy up throughout the day.

→ Lunch and dinner do not have to be rushed – try to slow down a little.

→ You can eat desserts, but try to make your own.

→ It's important to keep trying new recipes, meals, and foods!

So how can you make this all happen? With all of your new knowledge and help from reading labels, whether you're at home, at the store, at school or eating out, you're about to get some great ideas for not just thinking about good nutrition, but living it for real! So turn the page and let's make it happen.

MAKING IT HAPPEN — KEEP IT UP!

now that you've got a really good idea about how to prepare healthy meals and snacks for yourself, let's take a look at some ways that you can make good nutrition happen in the long term. It is important to get into the habit of eating healthy all the time, not just for a few meals or a few days a week. Deciding to commit to healthy eating is a lifetime goal.

Now let's look at some great ideas for making it happen!

In Your Home

If you and your family are all on the same "healthy eating" team, then good nutrition on a long-term basis will be so much easier. You can plan meals together, you can exercise together, and you can eat together. Eating with your family can be a lot of fun – you can talk about your day, hear everyone else's stories, and just unwind. If you can, try to make family mealtime a regular thing in your home.

Fast Bite

BIRDS OF A FEATHER EAT TOGETHER!

It turns out that you are more likely to eat more fruits and vegetables (YUM) and generally make healthier food choices when you eat at home with your family. So, whenever you can, eat with your family for at least one meal a day.[1]

145

Food Guides to Guide You

now that you have all kinds of info about macros, micros, labels, and how to plan a meal, you can see that it is actually pretty easy to eat well. You can make it even easier by combining that info with info about the food pyramid and the food groups.

Government health experts want their citizens to be healthy. So, these experts set goals and create food guidelines to ensure that people get what they need. Check out page 183 of the resource guide to find the website of your country's food guide.

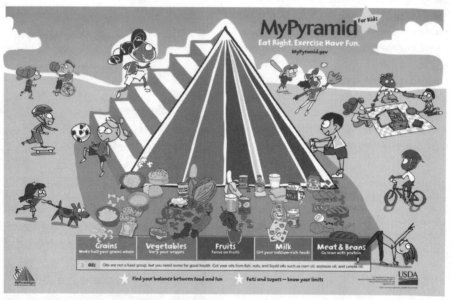

The US food pyramid for kids. Source: USDA Center for Nutrition Policy and Promotion

Good Idea!

Print out your food guide and keep it on the fridge in the kitchen so you can read it whenever you're preparing a meal or snack.

The food groups in the food guides can be really helpful when you want to keep creating healthy meals. Once you have tried the meal plans from this book, you can start changing the parts of your meal while keeping it packed with nutrients. And it's all with the help of your handy food guides!

↪ Don't feel like having 2 pancakes for breakfast? Switch those pancakes for 2 whole grain waffles, or 1/2 of a muffin.

↪ Not in the mood for an apple for your snack? Try 1/2 cup (125 mL) of pineapple or 1/2 of a papaya instead.

↪ Don't feel like having chicken with lunch? Have 2 oz (60 g) of crab meat or 2 Tbsp (25 mL) of nut butter on your whole grain bread.

↪ Not feeling like having milk with supper today? Go for 1 cup (250 mL) of fortified soy milk, or 3/4 cup of yogurt (175 mL) instead.

Once you've become a meal-planning pro, you might want to branch out and create entirely new meals and snacks. Your food guide can help you with this too! In order to make sure that you get what your body needs, think about it like this:

↪ Grains & cereals
   Macros: Energy, carbohydrates (especially fiber)
   Micros: B vitamins

↪ Fruits & vegetables
   Macros: Fiber
   Micros: Vitamins and minerals

↪ Milk & milk products
   Macros: Protein
   Micros: Vitamin D and calcium

↪ Meats & alternates
   Macros: Protein
   Micros: Iron and zinc

↪ Fats & oils
   Macros: Unsaturated fat
   Micros: Vitamin E

When you know this much about nutrition, the sky is the limit when it comes to creating healthy meals and snacks!

'OOD SAFET

Eating bugs is okay (if you haven't already heard, moths can be really tasty – check out page 41), but there are certain bugs, ones you can't even see, that are really bad for your body. When a person eats food that contains these bad bugs, it is called "food poisoning." Symptoms of food poisoning include a stomachache, diarrhea, and headache. Sometimes the food poisoning is so bad that a person has to go to the hospital to get medicine in order to feel better.

Bugs that cause food poisoning can grow on foods that are not kept at the right temperatures. This means that hot food should be kept hot (like on the stovetop, or in a Thermos for school lunches) and that cold food should be kept cold (like in the fridge, freezer, or in your lunch box with an ice pack). Sometimes, the smell of a food will let you know that it has gone bad (see page 92 for more info about that). But other times, the bad bugs don't create a smell. This means that you have to watch how long foods are stored in the fridge, in the freezer, and in your lunch box so that you don't eat something that's past its prime. If you're not sure how fresh something is, ask your parent(s).

Just as there are rules in sports, there are rules to preparing, serving, and storing foods. Here are more tips for safely preparing, serving, and storing foods:

→ Once you wash your hands, wash all fresh fruits and vegetables well before preparing them.

→ Hot foods should be kept hot (they should be kept at 140° F (60° C) or hotter) and cold foods should be kept cold (they should be kept at 39° F (4° C) or colder).

→ Seal and refrigerate (or freeze) any leftover food right after meals have been served.

→ Defrost frozen foods in the refrigerator – not on the kitchen counter – overnight.

→ Don't keep cooked food in your fridge for more than a couple of days.

Did You Know?

There is a whole other kind of food safety: you need to know that your food is free from chemicals from pollution in the environment. For example, the meat from large fish, like tuna and shark, may contain levels of mercury or other toxins that are not safe to eat.

In order to know which fish are safe to eat, check the Health Canada or the American Food and Drug Administration website in the resource pages at the back of this book.

TAKING IT EVEN FURTHER: GROW, GROW, GROW YOUR OWN

Growing your own herbs or vegetables is a great way to have delicious food on hand. Also, it's pretty cool to be able to eat something that you've grown yourself.

To get going, plan out where your garden could be and how much space you have to work with: will it be a couple of small containers on a windowsill? On the roof of your apartment building? Do you have a sunny spot in your backyard? Double-check with your parent(s) to make sure your plan is okay with them.

Once you've got a sense of your gardening space, go to your local gardening center (or talk to your family – maybe there's a gardener in the house!) and find out what can grow in your area. Choose seeds for veggies, fruits, and herbs that you really want. Don't forget to water them and feed them with plant food, choosing the most environmentally safe fertilizers. How cool is that – having your own "convenience" store so close to home?

WORMS LOVE LEFTOVERS

A vermicomposter is a box that you fill with dirt, leftovers from plant-based foods, and red wiggler worms. The worms eat the leftovers, and their poop mixes in with the dirt. If you separate the poop-dirt from the worms, you get an incredibly rich potting soil that the stuff in your garden will love!

Vermicomposters do require a fair bit of work – it's almost like having a cat or a dog, as the worms require daily care. But if this is something that interests you, check out our resources pages for more info.

In your Grocery Store

Let's go shopping!

When you shop for your food, you are choosing the ingredients for your meals and snacks. Whether you go to a huge supermarket, or to a small grocery store, what you buy will have a huge impact on your health. This is one of the most important steps in keeping healthy.

Wait a minute – that's not on my list!

A grocery list keeps you and your family organized during your trip to the store. When you shop with a list, you'll avoid getting stuck without an important ingredient for a supper dish, and you'll avoid buying stuff that you probably don't need.

Make a list at home with your parents, and take it with you to the grocery store. Plan it, list it, then buy it. Think about breakfast, lunch, and supper ideas, and then what types of snacks you need.

Getting it Ripe

Sometimes, you might bring home a fruit or vegetable that is not quite ripe, or ready to eat. While you can wait a few days for it to ripen naturally, why not work a little food magic and ripen it more quickly? The key to this trick is that all fruits and veggies emit a gas as they ripen, which can cause other produce to ripen.

Let's say you have bought an avocado and you want it to ripen quickly. Put it in a brown paper bag with a banana and close up the bag (a banana is a good choice here because it creates a lot of this gas). Inside the bag, the banana gas triggers the avocado to ripen a lot faster than it would have if you had let it ripen on its own.

THE SHOPPING LIST

First, start out with the key foods that should be on the pantry shelves and in your fridge so that there's always something great to eat:

Grains:
→ whole wheat flour, brown rice, oats, quinoa, multi-grain pasta, whole grain bread, and whole grain crackers (a low-salt variety).

Fruits:
→ any fresh fruit, frozen berries (blueberries, raspberries) are a good option, especially for smoothies. If you buy canned fruit, stick with those packed in a fruit juice, not in a syrup.

Veggies:
→ any fresh vegetable, frozen vegetables (peas, corn, beans, spinach, and edamame) are also a great option. If you buy canned veggies, stick to the brand that has the lowest amount of sodium.

Meat/fish/chicken/eggs/tofu/beans:
→ frozen lean beef, frozen salmon or trout, sole, canned tuna or salmon; chicken thighs or breast (skinless); carton of eggs; firm or soft tofu; canned beans (rinse well before you eat them) or dried beans.

Nuts and seeds:
→ jars of different nut butters (peanut, cashew, hazelnut, or mixtures); pumpkin seeds, sunflower seeds, peanuts, almonds, and cashews.

Milk and dairy:
→ 1, 2%, or 3.25% milk; cheese; soy or almond milk.

Others:
→ olive oil, canola oil, safflower oil.

Keep in mind that there are some things, like fruits and veggies, that you will have to buy more than once a week – remember that fresher always tastes better. Pick the fruits without the bruises or cuts – they can spoil quickly and make the rest of your chosen fruits go rotten too.

And while your list should have some of the foods on this page, what about trying something new? There are so many different tastes and flavors to enjoy. Try that star fruit or papaya when they are in season. How about trying a different kind of mushroom in a rice salad?

Did You Know?

Fruits are the fleshy parts of plants that are edible and that have seeds. Vegetables are also the fleshy parts of plants that can be eaten, but they contain no seeds. So, this means that tomatoes, cucumbers, squashes, and peppers (YUM!) are all actually fruits. We often think of them as vegetables because they are eaten with a meal, as opposed to fruits, like apples, oranges, and kiwis (YUM!), which are sweeter and are usually eaten after a meal, or as a snack.

Back in 1900, people actually fought about whether or not the tomato was a vegetable or fruit! At that time, veggies from other countries were being brought to the United States more and more frequently. The government wanted to keep this under control because they wanted to make sure that local farmers could still sell their vegetables. So, people who brought veggies into the United States were forced to pay high taxes. Many people who didn't want to pay these taxes complained that the tomato is actually a fruit and did not have to be taxed as a vegetable. The case went all the way to the Supreme Court, and the judge decided that even though a tomato is technically a fruit, people think of it more as a vegetable.[2] Poor tomato – who would think that produce could have an identity crisis?

Fast Bite

The next time you go to the supermarket with your parents, buy a fruit or vegetable that you've never tried before. Ask someone who works in the produce section about whether or not it is ripe, and ask for some suggestions about how to prepare it.

Also, check out the "Fruits and Veggies Matter" website: http://www.fruitsandveggiesmatter.gov/month/index.html This website highlights a different fruit and vegetable each month and provides great recipes for how to prepare them.

IT'S A JUNGLE IN THERE!

Once you get inside a supermarket, it can get pretty crazy – you have hundreds, maybe even thousands of products to choose from (which is why your list helps!). But there is a little secret to how to move around in any grocery store to ensure that you are getting some of the best, freshest stuff they have: stay on the edges of your supermarket and stay close to the doors. Here's why: when the fresh food arrives, employees have to rush to put it out on shelves that are close by, so that the food doesn't go bad. This means that they keep the fruits, veggies, dairy, meats, poultry, and fish products as close to their loading door as possible. The next time you're shopping, check out where the fresh foods are positioned in the store.

SEARCH HIGH AND LOW!

Once you get into the aisles, you are surrounded by all of the packaged foods. And because there are so many choices to make inside that grocery store, food manufacturers try their best to make sure that you notice their product and buy it (after all, they are in the business to make money). Often, they'll use cartoon characters and bright colors on their labels and packaging to attract your attention. Some food companies use celebrities in their advertisements to convince you to buy their food once you get to the store.

The problem is that many if not most of these foods are junk foods. Have you ever read the ingredient list on a bag of chips or cheesy doodles? Some of the chemicals in there have names that are too long to pronounce! And now that you're a label-reading pro, you can see that these types of snacks are typically loaded with saturated fat, sodium, and / or sugar. Yikes!

Now, because the owners of the supermarket want to make money too, they often put those same foods at your eye level – that way, you're sure to see them, and maybe you'll ask your parent(s) to buy them for you. But keep your eyes moving up and down, and use what you know about macros, micros, and reading labels to find products that are both delicious *and* good for you.

A LONG, LONG TIME AGO....

people used to hunt and gather their food. Their supermarkets were the forests and fields, where they caught animals and picked berries, leaves, and roots. They did not have cars to get around, and there were many hungry, wild animals that roamed around those forests and fields too. People were active all day in order to survive, and their foods were completely natural – no trans fats or additives for them!

This means that people used a lot more energy and stayed fit more easily than we do today. Their bodies were working hard all the time.

So how can you make your trip to the supermarket a little healthier? If your parent(s) drive a car to get to the supermarket, ask them to park a little farther away from the store. Or, if your grocery store is close enough, consider walking there and taking the bus back home.

THE SHOWDOWN – CHOOSING FOODS

The time has come. You've found the aisle you were looking for and you're trying to figure out what crackers to buy. You've narrowed it down to two different boxes, both of which look really good. How do you choose between the two? Use what you now know about label reading!

Take a look at the two pretend labels from two different crackers (p. 155). Which one is a better source of the nutrients your body needs?

CRACKER A	CRACKER B
Ingredients Enriched wheat flour, vegetable oil shortening (vegetable, modified palm, modified palm kernel), sugar, high fructose corn syrup, salt, glucose-fructose, malt flour, sodium bicarbonate, ammonium bicarbonate, monocalcium phosphate, soya lecithin, soyabean oil and hydrogenated cottonseed oil, with TBHQ and citric acid, amylase, protease, papain, yeast, sour dough culture.	**Ingredients** Whole grain rye flour, whole grain wheat flour, whole grain oat flour, whole grain barley flour, yeast, malted oats, rye bran, oat flakes, mono- and diglycerides (natural emulsifiers), sea salt.
Per 5 crackers (22 g) Calories 80 Fat 4 g (6 %) Saturated 1 g (5 %) Trans fat 1 g Cholesterol 0 mg Sodium 135 mg Carbohydrate 10 g Fiber 0 g Sugars 1 g Protein 1 g Vitamin A 0 % Vitamin C 0 % Calcium 2 % Iron 4 %	Per 5 crackers (22 g) Calories 48 Fat 0 g (0 %) Saturated 0 g (0 %) Trans fat 0 g Cholesterol 0 mg Sodium 80 mg Carbohydrate 10 g Fiber 2 g 8 % Sugars 0 g Protein 2 g Vitamin A 2 % Vitamin C 0 % Calcium 2 % Iron 4 % Thiamine 4 %

* Note: no real cracker labels were hurt in the creation of these pretend labels!

When comparing labels, ask yourself questions about the info given:

Serving size: Are the two products' serving sizes the same? **Yes**

Nutrition label: Which one has more fiber? **Cracker B**
More protein? **Cracker B**
More vitamins? **Cracker B**
More minerals? **They have the same amounts of vitamins A & C, and the same amounts of calcium and iron, but Cracker B has a little thiamine**
Which one has less fat? **Cracker B**
Less sodium? **Cracker B**

Ingredient list: Which one has fewer additives? **Cracker B**
Less added sugar? **Cracker B** (Cracker A has sugar listed as its third ingredient)

So, in this case, it is pretty obvious that Cracker B has a lot more of the nutrients that your body needs and less of the nutrients and ingredients that you don't need.

While Cracker B is the healthier of these two choices, sometimes the healthier choice may not be so clear: some products are fortified with vitamins and minerals, which is great, but if you look at the rest of their nutrient counts, you'll see that they really do not have the quantity of macros that you need.

Also, sometimes you'll notice that you want to compare two products, but their serving sizes are different, which will make a big difference when it comes to their nutrient counts (if that happens, ask an adult to help you do the math to compare the two foods).

Finally, don't feel as if you have to always choose the healthiest product – for example, you can choose Cracker A occasionally, but try to choose Cracker B more often.

Q: WHAT'S THE DEAL WITH ORGANIC?

A: When a food is labeled "organic," it means that the fruit, vegetable, or grain has been grown without using chemicals called pesticides (these chemicals help to keep bugs off of the crops). Growers will sometimes use natural products for pest control, or they will use no method of pest control at all. If a processed food is labeled "organic," it means that it was made with ingredients that were grown organically. If your family chooses to buy organic foods, you should know that they're usually more expensive than non-organic foods.

When farmers do use pesticides on their crops, they have to follow strict regulations to ensure that their food is safe to eat. Also, the government tests non-organic foods often to make sure that they contain only very small amounts of leftover pesticide chemicals.

Whether or not you buy organic food is a choice that only you and your family can make.

TAKING IT EVEN FURTHER: EAT LOCAL

When you buy produce that is grown – or meat from animals that are raised – in local fields, your food will be fresh and your family's money will support farmers who live in your area. Also, when you buy food that is made locally instead of buying things made far away, less pollution is created (no trucks had to travel huge distances to get the food to your supermarket). Everyone wins!

Buying locally also means eating seasonally – you eat the foods that are available as the seasons change. Depending on where you live, different fruits and vegetables will be "in season" at different times: for example, if you live in the Northeastern United States or central Canada, fall is great for local apples and root vegetables, like potatoes, carrots, and beets. Summer is a ripe time for many different fresh fruits, like peaches, berries, plums, and cherries.

Check out the local markets close to where you live or find them in your local phone book. If you live in the United States, you can also check out the Local Harvest website, which allows you to enter your city and state and will give you all of the farmers' markets in your area. If you live in Canada, check out the Chef2Chef Culinary Portal to see where the farmers' markets are located in your province.

What's the freshest way to get your foods? Do the picking yourself! Depending on where you live, you might be able to go pick apples, strawberries, pumpkins, or corn. Check to see if there are any "pick-your-own" farms in your area.

KEEP IT CLOSE

Alisa Smith and James McKinnon made the decision that for one year, they would only eat food that came from within 100 miles (161 kilometers) of their apartment in Vancouver, British Columbia. This was a pretty bold decision to make, especially because they found out that produce typically travels 1,500 miles (2,414 kilometers) to get from a farm, to a grocery store, to your plate (that's almost the same distance between Washington DC and Denver, Colorado, or between Montreal, Quebec, and Regina, Saskatchewan!).[3]

You can find out more about Alisa and James's 100-mile diet at their website: http://100milediet.org

WHERE IN THE WORLD IS YOUR FOOD COMING FROM?

As you know, your food often travels from great distances to get to your home. But just how far? Find a continent map on the Internet that shows states, provinces, and cities, and print it out. Mark where you live on the map with a bright red dot.

For one day, find out exactly where all of your food comes from by reading all of the stickers on your fresh food (or if your produce doesn't have a sticker, go online to find out where the food usually comes from) and by reading the packaging of all of the processed foods that you eat.

IN YOUR SCHOOL

Think about it: you spend a big chunk of your day in school. You learn there, you play there, and you eat there. There are plenty of opportunities for you to make healthy choices. In Chapter 4, we discussed how to make healthy lunches and snacks, and while you may usually bring your food with you to school, what if you don't?

VENDING MACHINES & CAFETERIAS
Different schools provide different foods for their students: some schools offer really healthy and fresh foods in their vending machines and in their cafeterias. Other schools have vending machines full of junk food, and cafeterias that serve a lot of greasy food.[4] As students, parents, and governments are pushing for schools to provide healthier food choices, a lot of schools are shaping up. Where does your school stand when it comes to healthy eating?

GYM CLASS
Gym is a fantastic subject in school – you get to play sports, run around, and work off any stress from your day. However, many schools have cut back the number of hours that their students have in the gym. When you do have gym class, you might not be active the whole time: when you factor in arriving to class late, listening to the teacher's instructions, and chatting with your friends, how much exercise are you really getting? And, even if your gym class does run super efficiently, sometimes you will be doing more strenuous cardio activities and sports, like basketball, while other times you will do less strenuous activities, like juggling or fencing.

TAKING IT EVEN FURTHER: TAKE ACTION

Take a look at your school and see if you can find answers to these questions:

Vending machines:
Are there vending machines in my school? How many?
Are there fresh foods available in these vending machines? If not, what kinds of foods are available?

Cafeteria:
What are the main meal choices in the cafeteria? Are they high or low fat? Do they offer a vegetarian option?
Are any fresh fruits or veggies being served?

Gym:
What kinds of activities do I do in my gym class?
Am I doing my best to stay active while I am in gym class?

The next step is totally up to you. You might decide to write a polite letter to your principal about the unhealthy food that is offered in the vending machines or about why you only have a half hour of gym every week. Or you might write a thank you letter for all of the healthy choices that are available in your cafeteria.

Our resource pages offer several sites that show you what other kids and teens have done to make their schools healthier. They're really inspiring!

WHAT CELEBS SAY

NFL player Tony Parrish:

"[I indulge myself] maybe once a week – or twice. It's hard to stay away. But if I start craving junk food, it means I'm hungry and I should eat some real food. Once I eat that, I don't want sweets anymore.[5]

ALLIES IN ACTION

Not only is it a great idea to get an adult's help when you're chopping, blending, and baking in the kitchen, but it's also awesome to have an adult help when it comes to bigger food issues, like the quality of food that's offered in your school.

In Canada, Paul Finkelstein, who used to be a professional chef, is now a teacher at a high school in Stratford, Ontario. Not only has he helped students create a 3,000-square foot (279-square meter) organic vegetable garden, but he also runs the Screaming Avocado Café. In the café, his students prepare fresh, healthy alternatives to the food offered in their school's cafeteria. The menus have included such delicious choices as rabbit braised in white wine with olives, crispy frog legs with a Thai noodle salad, and daily sushi selections.

In 2005, professional chef Jamie Oliver challenged himself: he wanted to show that he could feed 15,000 school kids in Greenwich, England, really healthy food for the same price as buying them each a bag of potato chips. Not only did he manage to do it (with a lot of help from the local lunch ladies!), but he has also influenced the British government to set up tough laws about having healthy foods in Britain's schools.

These are some true food champions.

EATING OUT

When you go out to eat, whether it is at a restaurant, a friend's house, or any other place that serves food, it can get a little tougher to eat healthy. But there are all kinds of things you can do to make delicious, smart choices.

SERVING SIZES

While the occasional trip to a favorite restaurant is okay, eating out a few times a week makes it difficult to keep your body balanced. In fact, the size of a typical fast food meal can be so high in calories that it can make up over 1/2 of your total energy needs for one whole day! How does that work? Well, the amount of food served in restaurants is often much bigger than what is recommended as a serving in the food guides. In some restaurants, you get 2 - 4 servings of pasta on one plate of spaghetti. Also you already know that fast food is usually loaded with saturated fat, sodium, and simple sugars, which all hit your body really hard.

So, when you're out for a meal, before you order, you can politely ask an employee how much pasta or how much meat is served in a particular meal. Based on what they tell you, you can make a more informed choice about your meal.

One you get your meal, if you see that there is way more food than you actually need, you can share the meal with your family, or you can bring some of it home to eat for another meal. That way, you can enjoy it twice!

SUGAR AND SALT

You might be surprised to see how much sugar and salt are in some fast foods. Check this out: Just how much sugar is in some drinks and some foods?

1 iced cupcake = 16 teaspoons (64 grams) sugar
12 oz (360 mL) can of soda pop = 10 teaspoons (40 grams) of sugar
1 doughnut, with glaze = 6 teaspoons (24 grams) sugar
Small, 1 oz (35 gram) chocolate bar = 5 teaspoons (20 grams) sugar
1 package of sweet-and-sour sauce = 3 teaspoons (11 grams) of sugar
1/2 cup (125 mL) frozen yogurt = 3 teaspoons (11 grams) sugar

Now check this out: Just how much salt is in some foods? (Remember that you're only supposed to eat about 1,200 - 1,500 mg of sodium per day.)
1 tsp (5 mL) salt = 2,325 mg of sodium
1 medium hot dog = 638 mg sodium
1 slice processed cheese = 406 mg sodium
1 Tbsp (15 mL) ketchup = 120-190 mg sodium
1 Tbsp soy sauce = 1,029 mg sodium
1 Tbsp (15 mL) soy sauce 40 % reduced salt = 600 mg sodium
Fresh foods like eggs, plain oatmeal, fish, chicken, and air-popped popcorn have very little sodium.

DECISIONS, DECISIONS

Eating out is a lot of fun. It's a great way to try different foods and different flavors. There are easy ways to pick the tastier and healthier choices, depending on the cuisine you are eating. Here are a few good picks from a few types of popular restaurant cuisines:

Burger places:
→ Choose a burger with a single patty, ask to have your burger plain, and then put on your own condiments.
→ Don't forget to order salad or cut-up veggies with about 1 to 2 Tbsp of salad dressing on the side (you don't need to make it soupy!).
→ Drink water or choose milk or a small-sized chocolate milk.

Sandwich & sub shops:
→ Choose whole grain bread.

→ Skip the butter or mayo, or ask the server to use only a little.
→ Ask for extra veggies.
→ Choose the lower-fat meats, like chicken breast or lean roast beef.

Pizza places:
→ Try a thin, whole grain crust.
→ Ask for extra veggies.
→ Choose grilled chicken instead of pepperoni.

Chinese food restaurants:
→ Ask for steamed rice instead of fried rice.
→ Get lots of steamed veggies.
→ Go for more grilled and less fried foods (try to stay away from the breaded shrimp and get the shrimp in garlic sauce instead).
→ Think about choosing Thai or Szechuan restaurants instead, which usually offer more steamed food choices than traditional Chinese restaurants.

KEEP YOUR EYES ON THE PRIZE (AND ON THE MOVIE!)

Going to the movies is such a fun way to spend an afternoon or an evening, but be careful when you approach the snack bar – candy, chocolate, chips, hot dogs, popcorn with butter, and massive soft drinks are among just a few of the different foods you have to chose from. Try these tips to make a healthy choice:

⊕ Bring or buy a bottle of water to keep your thirst at bay; if you decide you'd rather have a soda as a treat, buy the smallest size so that you don't get loads and loads of sugar and caffeine.

⊕ Share a medium-sized unbuttered popcorn with a friend.

⊕ If you're craving some candy, try to get the smallest package of candy they offer.

⊕ Remember that if you do buy a snack, you don't need to eat everything at the movie theater – save some of your candy or popcorn for tomorrow.

THE BUZZZZZZ ABOUT CAFFEINE

Caffeine occurs naturally in some foods, while in others, it is added. Found naturally in the coffee tree (used to make coffee), the cocoa plant (used to make chocolate), and the kola nut (often added to sodas), it is a chemical that makes the heart beat faster within 5 - 30 minutes of drinking or eating it. Sodas, even clear ones, can have caffeine.

If you limit sodas to special occasions and eat chocolate in moderation, then you won't get all buzzzzzed up and you'll be better able to get through your buzzzzzzy day. However, if you get too much caffeine, you will have trouble sleeping, which will lower your energy level for the next day (this also holds true for adults who drink too much coffee!).

How much is too much? Kids shouldn't get more than 62-85 mg of caffeine a day according to one government organization.[6] That's the amount in about 1/2 of an extra-large soft drink. Check out the drinks and foods below to keep your caffeine buzzzzz to a minimum.

Instant tea: 8 fl. oz. (250 mL) = 15 mg
Regular soda: 12 fl. oz. (355 mL) = 36 - 46 mg
Chocolate milk: 8 fl. oz. (250 mL) = 8 mg
Milk chocolate candy: 1 piece (28 grams) = 7 mg
Chocolate pudding: 5 fl. oz. (150 mL) = 9 mg

So, to recap:

When you eat at home:
→ Try to eat with your family as often as possible.
→ For real variety, combine what you've learned about macros and micros with info from the food guide.
→ Make sure that you follow food safety rules to avoid getting food poisoning.

When you are shopping for food:
→ Plan it, list it, buy it.
→ Shop strategically in the store.
→ Compare labels to make choices that work for you.

When you're at school:
→ Figure out where your school stands on nutrition and exercise.

When you're eating out:
→ Watch those serving sizes when it comes to meals and snack foods.
→ Try to choose healthy meals that are steamed, grilled, and full of veggies.
→ Try saving some of your food for later!

Take your nutrition know-how a step further – there's always more to learn!

TAKING IT EVEN FURTHER: LEARN ABOUT HUNGER

It's really important for you to know all about how macronutrients and micronutrients affect your body, and how to prepare and choose healthy foods. However, it is also really important to know that there's a lot more to food than that: some people don't have the resources to buy or grow food for themselves and their families.

As a nutrition-savvy person, it makes sense for you to find out more about food issues like poverty and hunger. UNICEF's Voices of Youth site offers a great page on the Millennium Development Goals, which are goals that many countries are working toward to make the world a better place. The first of these goals is to eliminate extreme poverty and hunger. This site offers great information and advice on how to take action and get the word out about these issues: http://www.unicef.org/voy/explore/mdg/explore_2204.html

You can also turn to our resource pages to find other websites that deal with hunger and poverty at home and around the world.

So now you know what's in your food, how it gets into your body, and how to keep your body balanced. Now it's time to put everything you've learned into action! Healthy eating is a lifetime goal.

IT'S ALL UP TO YOU

When it comes to what you eat, you make the decisions. Whether that means saying yes to a high-calorie meal or to a big leafy salad, or saying no to a sugary snack or a serving of tofu, you need to be aware of the food choices you're making as you're making them. Does this mean that you have to become Captain Serious about nutrition and watch everything you eat like a hawk? Of course not! It just means that now that you know all of this stuff about nutrition, you've got to go out there and use it.

Let's say that you're at a friend's house, and he puts a chocolate double-fudge cake out on the counter and hands you a fork. You can choose to dig in and eat half of the cake in five minutes. Or, you can choose to say, "No, thanks. I'm all good." But

remember that you always have a variety of choices, not just one or two: why not ask to have a slice of cake to yourself? Or even just a bite to give it a taste? You can get pretty creative with your choices and often, it does not have to be an all-or-nothing situation.

Or let's say your hockey team won the championship game (congrats, by the way!) and you all go out for burgers and fries to celebrate. Do you beat yourself up for eating a high-fat meal? No way! Special occasions often revolve around big meals, so why deprive yourself? Eating out occasionally won't affect your nutritional "health" if you make smart food choices the rest of the time.

Finally, it's great to share what you know about nutrition with friends and family, but remember that what they choose to eat is exactly that – their choice. If they want to know more, they'll ask. And you never know – they may look at your colorful pasta salad or whole grain sandwich and ask, "How did you make that?" You may help them discover that eating healthy can be really tasty too!

So eat up and have fun – after all, we are talking about food. YUM!

Make a Pledge

To make sure something gets done, you usually make a list, or write it down, right? Well, to ensure that healthy eating becomes a part of your life now, make a pledge. Then follow up with the six-month challenge on the next page, which will give you precise steps to take to reach your goal of a happy, healthy, balanced YOU.

1. Grab a pen and a piece of paper.
2. Write out the following: I, [insert your name], agree to make healthy eating a part of my life.
3. Under that, write down:
    a. Your main reason for wanting to eat nutritious foods.
    b. That you will choose macro- and micro-rich foods as often as possible.
    c. That you will exercise regularly.
    d. That you will keep junk foods and empty calories to a minimum.
4. Sign the pledge and ask your parents to sign it too.
5. Display the pledge in your room or in the kitchen.
6. Stay true to your pledge to eat healthy foods and stay active.

The Six-Month Challenge

This six-month challenge will help you find and maintain your body balance, especially if you get your family to join in.

It's simple: do the steps in Month 1, then in Month 2, keep up the activities from Month 1 and add on the activities from Month 2. Continue this way through the six months and you're on your way to a happy, healthy, balanced body.

The Six-Month Challenge

Month 1:
➔ Organize your pantry and refrigerator and store the less healthy foods out of sight – save these only for treats once in a while.

➔ Print out the USDA MyPyramid or the Health Canada Food Guide depending upon where you live, and post it on your fridge.

Month 2:
➔ Keep up the steps from the previous month.

➔ Make thorough grocery lists that include all of the good nutrition basics.

➔ Make a point to have at least one fresh fruit and one fresh vegetable with your meals.

Month 3:
➔ Keep up the steps from the previous months.

➔ Try three new recipes (like the ones in this book!).

➔ Choose water, bubbly water, or milk to drink with your meals and snacks.

Month 4:

→ Keep up the steps from the previous months.

→ Get in at least one hour of exercise or activity a day (either by yourself or with friends and family).

→ Limit screen time to 1-2 hours per day, maximum.

Month 5:

→ Keep up the steps from the previous months.

→ Cook at home 3-4 times per week.

→ Try at least three new foods.

Month 6:

→ Keep up the steps from the previous months.

→ At least once this month, make healthy choices at restaurants (and either split your meal with someone you're dining with or ask for a doggie bag so that you can bring home leftovers).

→ Switch it up! Vary your food choices and exercise routine so that you keep things interesting – which means you'll be more likely to stay true to your pledge!

LABELS:
WHAT'S TO EAT?

The food label and the list of ingredients on food packaging helps you choose what you're going to buy or eat. You can decide if one food is a good source of nutrients, or you can compare two foods to see which one should be going into your belly!

Remember: look for a serving that provides 15% or more of your Daily Value of several nutrients (except for sodium and saturated fat)!

When looking at one label, ask yourself these questions:

⊖ What size is the serving? Is that a reasonable size for me?

⊖ What about carbs?

⊖ What about fiber?

⊖ What about fat?

⊖ What about protein?

So, is one serving of this food a good source of some macros?

→ Is it a good source of Vitamins A and C?

→ Is it a good source of calcium and iron?

→ How much sodium does it have?

→ Does the label list any other micros?

So, is one serving of this food a good source of some micros?

Is this is a healthy choice for me?

When comparing labels, ask yourself these questions:

Nutrition label:
Which one has more fiber? More protein? More vitamins? More minerals?
Which one has less fat? Less sodium?

Ingredient list:
Which one has fewer additives? Less added sugar?

EXERCISE: WHAT ARE YOU IN THE MOOD TO DO?

Whether you're in training for a particular sport, a couch potato, or somewhere in the middle, it's smart to find a variety of exercises that you like. That way, you won't get bored during your exercise time. Also, when you mix it up, you will use different muscles in your body, which is really important for good health. Remember to talk to your doctor before starting any new exercise program or activity.

There are so many different types of activities and you might want to switch things up from time to time, depending on how you feel. Here are some options to get you started:

GOING SOLO
If you feel like exercising by yourself, then you've got plenty of choices, including yoga, tai chi, ice skating, roller blading, and even turning up the music and dancing in your room! You can also do sports drills for soccer, tennis, or volleyball by yourself. In addition, there are Podcasts and DVDs that can guide you through a whole whack of different exercises.

PARTNERING UP
If you feel like spending time with your best friend or one of your siblings (or even one of your parents!) while you exercise, there are many options. You can play badminton, squash or tennis, bike, dance, ice skate, and do paired sports drills for soccer, or volleyball.

GROUPING TOGETHER
If you feel like doing activities as part of a group of people, or as a member of a team, there's lots to choose from. You could take part in gymnastics, martial arts, swimming lessons, basketball, baseball, hockey, soccer, softball, touch football, volleyball, and chase games, like tag.

And remember, some of these activities can be done in an "organized" way, like if you're a member on a school team or if you sign up for a class at your community center. They can also be done "pick-up" style with friends at recess, or after school with other kids at your community center or in your neighborhood.

No matter what activity you decide to do, remember to do it for one hour each day and try to stay in the "cardio range," where your breathing is heavy but you can still carry on a conversation easily.

WHAT TO DO?

If you're stuck and you can't decide which activity to do, write each activity out on a small piece of paper, fold each paper up, and put all the papers in an empty jar (your exercise jar!). Pick one piece of paper each day and do that activity.

Chapter 1: What's In Our Food Anyway? Part I

1. The Food and Drug Administration, "Nutrient Content Claims," http://www.cfsan.fda.gov/~dms/fdnewlab.html.

2. Health Canada, "Background Factsheet 4: A Closer Look at % Daily Value," http://www.hc-sc.gc.ca/fn-an/alt_formats/hpfb-dgpsa/pdf/label-etiquet/te_background-le_point_e.pdf.

3. L. Matlik et al. "Perceived Milk Intolerance is Related to Bone Mineral Content in 10-to 13-Year- Old Female Adolescents," Pediatrics 120 (2007): 669-677.

4. "American Academy of Pediatrics–Committee on Nutrition–Statement on Cholesterol," Pediatrics 90 (1992): 469-473; I. Aeberli and M.B. Zimmerman, "Dietary Intake and Physical Activity of Normal Weight and Overweight 6 to 14 Year Old Swiss Children," Swiss Med Wkly 137 (2007): 424-30; M. Schmidt et al. "Fast-Food Intake and Diet Quality in Black and White Girls: the National Heart, Lung, and Blood Institute Growth and Health Study," Arch Pediatr Adolesc Med 159 (2005): 626-31.

5. Nemours Foundation, "Learning about Fats," KidsHealth, http://www.kidshealth.org/kid/stay_healthy/food/fat.html.

6. "American Academy of Pediatrics – Committee on Nutrition – Statement on Cholesterol," Pediatrics 90 (1992): 469-473.; T. Lobstein, and R. Jackson-Leach, "Estimated Burden of Paediatric Obesity and Co-Morbidities in Europe, Part 2: Numbers of Children with Indicators of Obesity-Related Disease." Int J Pediatr Obes 1 (2006): 33-41.

7. A.E. Pagano, "Whole Grains and the Gluten-Free Diet," Practical Gastroenterology, Series 2, https://healthsystem.virginia.edu/internet/digestive-health/nutritionarticles/paganoarticle.pdf.

8. B. Handwerk, "Thanksgiving Mystery: Does Turkey Make You Sleepy?" National Geographic News, November 2005, http://news.nationalgeographic.com/news/2005/11/1122_051122_thanksgiving.html.

9. Worldwatch Institute, "Global Meat Consumption has Far-Ranging Environmental Impacts," http://www.worldwatch.org/node/1670.

10. E. O'Brien, "Moths Blanket Sydney Skyscrapers as Winds Blow Bugs Off Course," Bloomberg.com, http://www.bloomberg.com/apps/news?pid=20601080&sid=abT2WntLhGsY&refer=asia.

11. "Wildlife of Sydney: Bogong Moth Fact File," Australian Museum, http://www.faunanet.gov.au/wos/factfile.cfm?Fact_ID=204.

12. Professor B. Barry Levy, Department of Jewish Studies, McGill University, e-mail message to Lindsay Cornish, November 29, 2007.

Chapter 2: What's In Our Food Anyway? Part II

1. G. Wolf, "A History of Vitamin A and Retinoids," FASEB J: 9: 1102-7, 1996.

2. G. Wolf, "A History of Vitamin A and Retinoids," FASEB J: 9: 1102-7, 1996.

3. K.J. Carpenter, The History of Scurvy and Vitamin C (Cambridge, UK: Cambridge University Press, 1998).

4. K. Rajakumar, "Vitamin D, Cod-Liver Oil, Sunlight, and Rickets: A Historical Perspective," Pediatrics 112, no. 2 (August 2003):132-5.

5. L.S. Nield et al, "Rickets: Not a Disease of the Past," Am Fam Physician 74 (2006):619-26, 629-30.

6. Unite for Sight, "Vitamin A Deficiency – Xerophthalmia," http://www.uniteforsight. org/parents/vitamina.php.

7. W.C. Sherman and W.D. Salmon, "Carotene Content of Different Varieties of Green and Mature Soybeans and Cowpeas, J Food Sci 4 (1939): 371-80.

8. D.L. Fox, V.E. Smith, and A.A. Wolfson, "Carotenoid Selectivity in Blood and Feathers of Lesser (African), Chilean and Greater (European) Flamingos," Comp Biochem Physiol 23 (1967): 225-32.

9. E.M. Haymes, "Vitamin and Mineral Supplementation to Athletes," Int J Sport Nutr 1 (1991): 146-69.

10. H. Hemila and Z.S. Herman, "Vitamin C and the Common Cold: A Retrospective Analysis of Chalmers' Review," J Am Coll Nutr, 14, no. 2 (1995): 116-123.

11. Linus C. Pauling, Vitamin C and the Common Cold (San Francisco: W. H. Freeman, 1970).

12. O. Engelsen et al, "Daily Duration of Vitamin D Synthesis in Human Skin with Relation to Latitude, Total Ozone, Altitude, Ground Cover, Aerosols and Cloud Thickness Photochemistry and Photobiology," Photochem Photobiol 81 (2005): 1287-1290; M.F. Holick, "Vitamin D: The Underappreciated D-lightful Hormone that is Important for Skeletal and Cellular Health," Curr Opin Endocrinol Diabetes 9 (2002): 87-98; R. Vieth et al. "The Urgent Need to Recommend an Intake of Vitamin D that is Effective," Am J Clin Nutr 85 (2007):649-50.

13. "Dietary Supplement Fact Sheet: Vitamin D," Office of Dietary Supplements, NIH Clinical Center, National Institute of Health, http://ods.od.nih.gov/factsheets/vitamind.asp.

14. A.C. Chandler, "Vitamin D, The Sunshine Vitamin, and Other Fat-Soluble Vitamins" (1939), Rice University Digital Repository, Fondren Library, http://hdl.handle. net/1911/9097.

15. K.M. Labak, "Pet Reptiles Need Vitamin D and Calcium for Bone Health," College of Veterinary Medicine, University of Illinois at Urbana-Champaign, http://www.cvm.uiuc. edu/petcolumns/index.cfm?function=showarticle&id=425.

16. J.L. Groff, S.S. Gropper and S. Hunt, Advanced Nutrition and Human Metabolism, 2nd Ed. (St. Paul, MN: West Pub, 1995), pp. 325, 327, 353.

17. F.R. Greer, N.F. Krebs and the Committee on Nutrition, "Optimizing Bone Health and Calcium Intakes of Infants, Children and Adolescents," Pediatrics 117 (2006): 578-585.

18. J. Starkey et al., "Food Habits of Canadians: Comparison of Intakes in Adults and Adolescents to Canada's Food Guide to Healthy Eating," Canadian Journal of Dietetic Practice and Research, 62, no. 2 (2001):61-69.

19. D. Garriguet, "Sodium Consumption at All Ages," Statistics Canada Health Reports, http://www.statcan.ca/english/freepub/82-003-XIE/2006004/articles/sodium/sodiumconsumption_e.pdf

20. L.J. Appel, "Salt Reduction in the United States," BMJ 333 (2006): 561-2.

21. The Food and Drug Administration, "Nutrient Content Claims," http://www.cfsan.fda.gov/~dms/fdnewlab.html.

22. Health Canada, "Background Factsheet 4: A Closer Look at % Daily Value,"http://www.hc-sc.gc.ca/fn-an/alt_formats/hpfb-dgpsa/pdf/label-etiquet/te_background-le_point_e.pdf.

Chapter 3: The Amazing Body

1. J.L. Groff, S.S. Gropper and S. Hunt, Advanced Nutrition and Human Metabolism, 2nd Ed. (St. Paul, MN: West Pub, 1995): 423.

2. Dietitians of Canada, "Water for Health and Sport," Current Issues (April, 2006).

3. The Toronto Zoo, "Bactrian Camel," http://www.torontozoo.com/animals/details.asp?AnimalId=360.

4. J.A. Mennella et al., "Prenatal and Postnatal Flavor Learning by Human Infants," Pediatrics 107 (2001): 88-94.

5. B. Lindemann, "A Taste for Umami," Nature Neuroscience 3 (2000): 99-100, http://www.nature.com/neuro/journal/v3/n2/full/nn0200_99.html.

6. S. Bastin, "Mysteries of the Kitchen Revealed," College of Agriculture, University of Kentucky, http://www.ca.uky.edu/hes/fcs/factshts/FN-SSB.019.PDF.

7. L. Valette et al., "Volatile Constituents from Romanesco Cauliflower," Food Chem 80 (2003): 353-358.

8. G. Wilkes, "Hiccups," WebMed (August, 2007), http://www.emedicine.com/emerg/TOPIC252.HTM.

9. M.V. Krause and L.K. Mahan, Food, Nutrition and Diet Therapy. 6th Ed. (Phil, PA: WB Saunders,1979), p. 94.

10. V. Loening-Baucke and A. Swidsinski, "Constipation as a Cause of Acute Abdominal Pain in Children," Journal of Pediatrics 151 (2007): 666-669.

11. L. Jacobs Starkey et al, "Food Habits of Canadians: Comparison of Intakes in Adults and Adolescents to Canada's Food Guide to Healthy Eating," Canadian Journal of Dietetic Practice and Research 62, no. 2 (2001): 61-69.

12. D.A. Lemberg et al., "Probiotics in Paediatric Gastrointestinal Diseases," J Pediatr Child Health 43 (2007): 331-336.

13. The Nemours Foundation, "Kids and Exercise," Kids' Health, http://www.kidshealth.org/parent/nutrition_fit/fitness/exercise.html.

14. Canadian Broadcast Corporation, "Benefits of Exercise for Kids Goes Beyond Physical," http://www.cbc.ca/health/story/2005/06/13/exercise-kids050613.html.

15. R. Howard. "Without Dance, They'd Just Be ... Roni Mahler Brings Ballet to the Sports World." Dance Magazine (Jan 2004): http://findarticles.com/p/articles/mi_m1083/is_1_78/ai_112212780.

16. National Sleep Foundation, "What Happens When You Sleep," http://www.sleepfoundation.org/site/c.huIXKjM0IxF/b.2419159/k.A817/What_Happens_When_You_Sleep.htm.

17. National Sleep Foundation, "Sleep and You," Sleep for Kids, http://www.sleepforkids.org/html/you.html.

18. K. Boyse, "Sleep Problems," University of Michigan Health Systems, http://www.med.umich.edu/1Libr/yourchild/sleep.htm#childrens.

19. J. W. Blum et al. "Beverage Consumption Patterns in Elementary School Aged Children Across a Two-Year Period," J Amer Coll Nutr 24 (2005): 93-98.

20. Z. Jones, "HELLO my name is America Ferrera," Scholastic Action (September 2007): 4.

21. "Behind the Scenes," People (Summer 2007): 8.

22. J. Furmaniak, "Jessica Alba," Seventeen 66, no. 7 (July 2007): 88.

Chapter 4: Eating Well Throughout the Day

1. R.E. Kleinman et al., "Diet, Breakfast and Academic Performance in Children," Ann Nutr Metab 46 Suppl 1 (2002): 24-30.

2. C.R. Mahoney et al., "Effect of Breakfast Composition on Cognitive Performance in Elementary School Children," Physiol Behav 85 (2005): 635-45.

3. R.E. Kleinman et al., "Diet, Breakfast and Academic Performance in Children," Ann Nutr Metab 1 (2002): 24-30.

4. C.R. Mahoney et al., "Effect of Breakfast Composition on Cognitive Performance in Elementary School Children," Physiol Behav 85 (2005): 635-45.

5. C. Connors, "My 10 Rules for Healthy Living," Shape 26, no. 6 (February 2007): 43.

6. A.M. O'Connor, "How Stars Stay Slim," Shape 26, no.7 (March 2007): 192.

7. M. Brophy, "10 Things I Can't Live Without," Sports Illustrated for Kids 18, no.1 (January 2006): 49.

8. People (Summer 2004): 24.

9. S. Al-Muhsen, "Peanut Allergy: An Overview," CMAJ 168 (2003):1279-85.

10. S.H. Sicherer et al., "Prevalence of Peanut and Tree Nut Allergy in the United States Determined by Means of a Random Digit Dial Telephone Survey: A 5-Year Follow-up Study," J Allergy and Clinical

Immunology 112 (2003): 1203-1207.

11. B.A. Sparkes, "The Greek Kitchen," The Journal of Hellenic Studies 82 (1962): 121-137.

12. "Kicking It with Mia Hamm," Children's Digest 56, no. 6 (November/December 2007): 27.

Chapter 5: Making it Happen – Keep it Up!

1. N.I. Larson et al., "Family Meals During Adolescence are Associated with Higher Diet Quality and Healthful Meal Patterns During Young Adulthood," JADA 107 (2007): 1502-1510.

2. New Mexico State University, "Crop Plant Resources: Tomato," http://darwin.nmsu.edu/~molbio/plant/tomato.html/; J. Nix et al. v. E. Hedden, Collector of the Port of New York, 149 U.S. 304 (1893).

3. Hendrickson, John. 1996. "Energy use in the U.S. food system: A summary of existing research and analysis." Sustainable Farming-REAP-Canada. Ste. Anne-de'Bellevue, Quebec. Vol 7, No 4. Fall 1997.

4. "Policy on Healthy Foods and Beverages in Elementary School Vending Machines" (2004), Ontario Ministry of Education, http://www.edu.gov.on.ca/extra/eng/ppm/135.html.

5. N. Friedman, "Eating Like an NFL Pro," Sports Illustrated for Kids 17, no. 8 (January 2006): 22.

6. Health Canada, "It's Your Health: Caffeine," http://www.hc-sc.gc.ca/iyh-vsv/food-aliment/caffeine_e.html.

7. S.L. Hofferth and J.F. Sandberg, "How American Children Spend their Time," J Marriage Fam 63 (2001): 295-308.

General Information

United States:

USDA's MyPyramid Plan, http://www.mypyramid.gov/mypyramid/index.aspx. Customize the food pyramid to create a food plan just for you. See how many servings of food you should be eating per day.

Centers of Disease Control and Prevention: Bam! Body and Mind, http://www.bam.gov/sub_foodnutrition/index.html Find fun, healthy recipes, tips on packing the perfect lunch, and advice on eating at restaurants. You can even share your experiences with other kids.

KidsHealth's "Go, Slow, and Whoa!" http://www.kidshealth.org/kid/stay_healthy/food/go_slow_whoa.html The food pyramid is not the only way you can think about food categories. The U.S. National Heart, Lung, and Blood Institute provides a detailed list of "Go, Slow, and Whoa" food categories. These are based on what you can eat all the time ("Go"), sometimes ("Slow"), and once in a while ("Whoa"). Check out this site to learn more.

Canada:

Health Canada's My Food Guide, http://www.hc-sc.gc.ca/fn-an/food-guide-aliment/myguide-monguide/index_e.html Customize the Canadian food guide to suit your personal needs. Learn just how many servings of food you should be eating per day.

AboutKidsHealth! http://www.aboutkidshealth.ca/JustForKids/ This initiative by Toronto Ontario's Hospital for Sick Children tells you everything you want to know about your health and your body.

Healthy Eating is in Store for You™: Virtual Grocery Store, http://www.healthyeatingisinstore.ca/virtual_grocery.asp You can use your food-label smarts to make informed choices in this virtual supermarket. The Virtual Grocery Store is brought to you by a partnership between Dietitians of Canada and the Canadian Diabetes Association.

"Cafeteria Confidential," Marketplace, CBC News, http://www.cbc.ca/consumers/market/files/food/cafeteria/ Why are school cafeterias stocked with greasy pizza, caffeinated soft drinks, and other unhealthy food? Read about students who have had enough and are trying to put a stop to poor quality food in their cafeterias.

NutritionData™ Nutrition Facts & Calorie Counter, http://www.nutritiondata.com/ You can enter foods that don't come with food labels into this database to get the nutrition information you need. The information in Nutrition Data's database comes from the USDA's National Nutrient Database for Standard Reference and is supplemented by listings provided by restaurants and food manufacturers. The source for each individual food item is listed in the footnotes of that food's analysis page.

National Institutes of Health: Milk Matters, http://www.nichd.nih.gov/milk/kids/kidsteens.cfm Play these calcium games and find out why milk matters!

Plant a Row • Grow a Row, http://www.growarow.org/pargar_jr_main.htm Grow your own veggie garden with your family and enjoy fresh produce from your own backyard! Also, learn about composting – recycling organic material into a soil-like product – from your home.

The Body

Juvenile Diabetes Research Foundation International, http://kids.jdrf.org/ If you are living with diabetes, you are not alone. This site can help you manage your day-to-day diabetes, answer your questions, and help you connect with other kids who are also living with diabetes. This site provides tons of information and it can help non-diabetic kids understand what the disease is all about.

Food Allergy & Anaphylaxis Network (FAAN), http://www.faankids.org/
Learn about the foods kids are typically allergic to, symptoms of food allergies, how to treat these symptoms, and how to prevent you or your friends from having allergic reactions in the future.

Safe4Kids, www.safe4kids.ca
Kids living with anaphylaxis have life-threatening allergic reactions to certain foods. Learn how you and your friends can avoid the allergen that causes this reaction, play Safe Kids Trivia, solve the anaphylaxis crossword puzzle, and share your allergy artwork here.

Digestion, http://kitses.com/animation/swfs/digestion.swf
Check out this awesome animation to see how your body digests different kinds of food. This animation is designed for the British Broadcasting Corporation (©2001) by John Kitses.

United States:
You're It. Get Fit! http://www.fitness.gov/challenge/getfitandbeactive.pdf
Get fit with motivational tips, exercise guides, and other physical fitness advice. This online magazine is brought to you by the U.S. Department of Health and Human Services.

Exercise and Activities, http://www.verbnow.com/
Create your own original exercises, characters, and virtual playgrounds here. This exercise site has activities by kids, for kids, and it's brought to you by the U.S. Department of Health and Human Services Centers for Disease Control and Prevention.

Canada:
Let's Get Active, Public Health Agency of Canada, http://www.phac-aspc.gc.ca/pau-uap/paguide/child_youth/pdf/yth_magazine_e.pdf
Crank up your daily physical activity with this online magazine.

Mealtime

Recipes:
PBS's Café Zoom, http://pbskids.org/zoom/activities/cafe/ Cook up some Fabulous Fruit Kebabs, Butterfly Sandwiches, Homemade Applesauce, and other scrumptious, simple recipes.

"5-a-Day, The Color Way," http://www.5aday.org/html/recipes/onthemenu.php
The Produce for Better Health Foundation designed "5-a-Day, The Color Way" to help you become a top-notch healthy chef. The site's recipes promote cooking with vegetables, fruits, and whole grains.

"Fruit & Vegetable of the Month," http://www.fruitsandveggiesmatter.gov/month/index.html
Celebrate variety by cooking special recipes that feature the fruit and vegetable of the month! This easy-to-use website is brought to you by The Centers for Disease Control.

Food Safety

United States:
The USDA's "Safe Food Park," http://www.fsis.usda.gov/OA/foodsafetymobile/mobilegame.swf. Take an online ride through Safe Food Park and try to defeat the invisible enemy, BAC (Bacteria).

Canada:
Partnership for Food Safety Education, http://www.fightbac.org/images/pdfs/Grades4-8Experiments.pdf
Print out "All Washed Up," a PDF sheet of experiments that you and your friends can

do together to learn about different aspects of food safety.

And beyond...

Vermicomposting

The New Farm®, http://www.newfarm.org/features/0804/wormbin/index.shtml
Vermicomposting is the recycling of organic material with the help of worms. This site provides directions for taking composting to the next level.

Buy locally

"100-Mile Diet: Local Eating for Global Change," http://100milediet.org/
The "100-Mile Diet" is a local-eating challenge, where you eat food that comes from within 100 miles of your home. Check out this website to learn more about the benefits of locally grown and produced food.

Think Critically

"Get Outta My Face," http://www.get-outta-my-face.com/
This nonprofit group in the U.S. is comprised of kids who are "tired of being the fattest and most unfit generation ever." These kids are rallying against food advertising that targets kids like you. They've even launched a film contest for kids who want to make a statement against food advertisers.

PBS Kids: "Don't Buy It: Get Media Smart!" http://pbskids.org/dontbuyit/advertisingtricks/foodadtricks.html
Become media savvy by learning food advertising tricks that can make any food on television look mouth watering.

Media Awareness Network, http://www.media-awareness.ca/english/resources/educational/handouts/advertising_marketing/food_ads.cfm
See how food stylists use paint, deodorant, baby powder and other materials to make food look picture perfect.

Be Aware

United States:

Local Harvest, http://www.localharvest.org/organic-farms/
Learn how to support family-owned farms. This site can help you and your family find American farmers' markets, and restaurants that use fresh local foods.

Environmental Kids Club, Environmental Protection Agency (EPA), http://www.epa.gov/kids/water.htm
Learn about hunger, poverty, recycling, and water issues around the world and find out what you can do to help.

America's Second Harvest: The Nation's Food Bank Network: www.secondharvest.org
America's Second Harvest is the nation's largest charitable hunger-relief organization. Help create a hunger-free America here.

United Nations Children's Fund's "The Voices of Youth," http://www.unicef.org/voy/explore/mdg/explore_2204.html
This organization is dedicated to making sure youth can do more about the world they live in. Learn how to take action and speak out.

Canada:

Chef2Chef Culinary Portal: Links to Canadian Farmers Markets, http://marketplace.chef2chef.net/farmer-markets/canada.htm
Use this site to find farmers' markets close to you.

Oxfam (Canada), http://www.oxfam.ca/youth-students
Oxfam is dedicated to "building lasting solutions to global poverty and injustice." Join Oxfam's Youth and Student program to learn how you can volunteer.

Absorption: the process that occurs when the smallest parts of foods (monosaccharides, fatty acids, amino acids, vitamins, and minerals) are moved across the wall of the intestines and into the blood during digestion.

Allergy: Sometimes, people's bodies react to a food (or other substances in the environment, like dust, pet dander, etc.) as though the substance were a poison to the body. This is called an allergy. When the body is exposed to that food, the immune system kicks in to protect the body. This can cause many different symptoms, including small swellings on the skin (called hives), indigestion, and even vomiting. The most severe allergic reaction that a person can have is called anaphylaxis, which can make it difficult for someone to breathe. Kids with nut and peanut allergies are at high risk of having this type of reaction, and they have to carry medication with them at all times. This medication is kept in a special spring-loaded needle called an Epipen, which contains a powerful allergy medicine that will help them breathe if they have a severe reaction.

Almond milk: milk that is made from ground almonds. Almond milk does not have any cholesterol or lactose so it is a good choice for someone who is lactose intolerant. Almond milk may be fortified with added minerals and vitamins.

Amino acids: the building blocks of protein: several amino acids are strung together to create a full protein molecule. When the body digests protein, it breaks them down into amino acids, which are then used by the body for many things, like to build body structures, including your bones, hair, skin, teeth, and nails.

Anorexia nervosa: an eating disorder where someone severely limits the amount of food they are eating on purpose. The person may also exercise for long periods of time in an effort to continue losing weight. When a person has anorexia, their body suffers because it is not provided with enough energy or nutrients. Not only can someone become very underweight, but their heart can become weaker and they can get sicker more easily. People with anorexia sometimes have bulimia too. While anorexia strikes girls more often than it strikes boys, anyone with anorexia needs help from a medical doctor or other health professional in order to get better.

Antioxidants: protect cells from being damaged by waste materials from cell reactions. Vitamins C and E are examples of antioxidants.

Binge eating: an eating disorder when a person eats abnormally large amounts of food at one time, and often in secrecy so that other people do not see them do it. Binge eating can cause a person to have too much body fat, which can cause serious health problems. When a person has bulimia, they binge eat, but then they get the food out of their body by throwing up or using medications. As with other eating disorders, someone who has a problem with binge eating should seek help from a medical professional to get better. See anorexia nervosa.

Body Mass Index: a way to figure out if someone's body size is in a healthy range for their age and height. While there are Body Mass Index (BMI) tools online, the best way to determine your BMI is to have your doctor figure it out.

Bulimia: an eating disorder where someone eats a huge amount of food at one time (binge eating), then tries to get rid of it by throwing up or using medications to make them go to the bathroom. Someone with bulimia may also alternate between bulimic behavior and anorexia-type behavior (limiting how much and what they eat very severely, and often regularly exercising for very long periods of time). While bulimia strikes girls more often than it strike boys, anyone with bulimia needs help from a doctor and a psychologist in order to get better.

Calorie: a unit used to measure the amount of energy in a serving of food, how much energy a person needs, or how much energy a person uses. Calories that we read about are actually kilocalories, but because the calorie unit is so small, people rarely say "kilo" before "calories."

Carotene (also called beta carotene): a form of vitamin A that is not active. It has to be made into vitamin A once it's in the body. Carotene is a carotenoid, which is the red or yellow pigment in fruits and vegetables.

Cholesterol: a fat-like substance in the blood. The body makes its own cholesterol and it gets cholesterol from digested food too. Foods that have cholesterol include eggs, shrimp, butter, meat, and chicken. If cholesterol levels in the blood go too high, then that can affect the health of someone's heart.

Complex carbohydrates: carbohydrates made of long chains of simple sugars. When the body digests complex carbohydrates, it breaks these long chains so that the body can absorb these simple sugars. Because complex carbohydrates are broken down more slowly than other carbohydrates (like monosaccharides and disaccharides), they are a longer-lasting source of energy. One complex carbohydrate that's really important to digestion is fiber, which the body cannot break down. Complex carbs are also called polysaccharides.

Complete protein: a protein that has all of the amino acid building blocks for growth and development that people need. Eggs, milk, meat, chicken, fish, and quinoa are considered to be complete proteins.

Cravings: the strong desire to eat a specific food.

Daily Value: the amount of a nutrient that is recommended, usually based on a 2,000-calorie diet. When a food label indicates a % DV of a nutrient, the amount in the food is compared to the amount of that nutrient that is recommended every day. The % DV helps people decide if a food is a high or low source of a nutrient. While % DV is based on an adult's consumption of calories, it is still really useful to help kids figure out whether a serving of food is a good source of a nutrient.

Diabetes: when a person's body either doesn't make insulin, or when their body can't use the insulin that they make, they are considered diabetic. When this happens, the body can't use sugar for energy. The sugar floats around in the bloodstream, which can make a person really sick in the long-run. However, people with diabetes can take insulin injections or pills that help their bodies use sugar for energy and they can live very healthy lives. People with diabetes who take insulin have to be especially careful to eat well and to eat at regular times, including about the same amounts of carbohydrate at each meal and snack. This is important so that their blood sugar does not go too high or too low with the insulin.

Diaphragm: a large muscle that separates your chest from your abdomen (the abdomen is where you find the stomach, intestines, liver, and other organs). The diaphragm is the main muscle that helps you to breathe.

Dietitian: someone who has gone to university to study all aspects of nutrition and healthy eating. Part of a dietitian's learning involves being trained in a hospital and a community setting, where they help people who are not well to choose the right foods to help them get better. Dietitians work in hospitals, as well as in the government, for food companies, for school boards, and in health offices.

Digestion: the process that the body uses to break down food into smaller units that can be used by the body. It involves physically breaking food down (by chewing and grinding) and chemically breaking food down (by digestive juices).

Disaccharides: a carbohydrate that is made up of two monosaccharides ("di" means "two"). Like monosaccharides, they are simple sugars. Lactose is a disaccharide made up of two monosaccharides, glucose and galactose. See also: Lactose intolerance.

Edamame: beans from the soy plant that are a good source of fiber, protein, and iron. They are typically found in the frozen food section of supermarkets and they can be bought with or without the shell.

Enriched: like fortification, when a food has had vitamins or minerals added to increase the nutritional value of that particular food. Enriching foods is usually done when nutrients are lost during processing, while fortification may be to add more of a nutrient to a food whether or not it was ever there. The government sets regulations on which foods and what nutrients can be used to enrich foods.

Enzymes: proteins that make important chemical reactions happen inside your cells. They also do important jobs outside of your cells: for example, enzymes play a role in breaking down your food so that it can be absorbed into your bloodstream.

Essential fatty acids: Omega-3 and omega-6 fatty acids are necessary, because if they are not taken in through the diet, then someone may grow poorly and have skin rashes. Foods like juice, milk, and breads are often enriched or fortified with omega-3 because people are not getting enough of the essential fatty acids in other foods they eat.

Fatty acids: the single units that are the building blocks for fat. Fatty acids are used by the body for energy, for storage, and for building parts of cells, like the cell walls. Healthy fats, like the polyunsaturated fats in nuts, seeds, and vegetable oils, keep fat levels in the blood healthy.

Fiber: a complex carbohydrate that the human body can't digest. It can be found in fruits, veggies, grains, legumes, and nuts. Fiber helps your poops stay soft and easy to pass; it also helps to keep your blood sugar and cholesterol levels within a healthy range.

Flax: a type of plant with seeds that you can eat. Flaxseeds are high in omega-3 essential fatty acids. Your body cannot digest a whole flaxseed, so when you use them in your food, you need to grind them up to break down the hard seed coat (a coffee grinder is great for this). You can add ground flaxseeds to yogurt, pancakes, and salads. You should store ground flaxseeds in a sealed container in your fridge or in your freezer to keep them fresh.

Food poisoning: a flu-like condition caused by a harmful bug in a person's food. Symptoms of food poisoning include vomiting, diarrhea, terrible stomachaches, and headaches. To avoid getting food poisoning, it's helpful to keep foods at the right temperature and to avoid eating foods that have been in the fridge or freezer for too long. In severe cases of food poisoning, someone may have to go to the hospital for treatment.

Gut flora: the microorganisms that live in the small and large intestines. These important bugs keep your immune system healthy and strong, and together, they stop bad bugs from getting inside your body.

Hormones: proteins that send messages from one group of cells to another with instructions for what the cells should do. One of the important hormones in your body is insulin, which is made in your pancreas. Insulin helps to get sugar into cells so that they can use it for energy.

Immune system: a group of cells and organs in your body that protects your body from illness. The immune system includes your tonsils, the appendix, parts of your small intestines, and your blood. When bad bugs, viruses, or other invaders get into your body, the different parts of your immune system work together to get rid of them. Once an invader is spotted, the immune system goes into action to get rid of it and stop it from trying to hurt you again. Antibodies like immunoglobulins are examples of proteins of the immune system.

Incomplete protein: a protein that does not have all the essential amino acids to make a complete protein. The protein found in most vegetables and grains are incomplete proteins.

Insulin: a hormone made by the pancreas that helps get digested sugar into your body's cells. Under normal circumstances, insulin keeps the level of sugar in the bloodstream in a healthy range. When a person has diabetes, either their pancreas makes no insulin at all, or their body can't use the insulin that it makes properly.

Lactose intolerance: when the body can't break down a disaccharide called lactose, which is found in milk and dairy products. When people who are lactose intolerant drink milk, their body does not have enough of the enzyme (called lactase) to break down the lactose, which results in a stomachache, bloating, gas, and even diarrhea. This can be a temporary condition brought on by a stomach virus. If milk is gradually brought back into the person's diet, their body will slowly start making the needed enzyme again. It can also be a long-term problem, in which case a person can buy milk products that are already treated with the needed enzyme, or they can choose soy milk and other plant-based milks, like rice milk, instead.

Legumes: the fruit part of a plant that is edible and that is contained in a pod that splits open. Legumes include beans and peas, such as lentils, chickpeas, and peanuts, and are generally a very good source of fiber, protein, and iron.

Macronutrients: the three main parts of food – carbohydrate, protein, and fat – that the body needs in large quantities for growth and development.

Micronutrients: The smaller parts of foods, including the vitamins and minerals that the body needs in small quantities for growth and development.

Monosaccharides: the single units that are the building blocks of carbohydrates. Your body breaks down all carbohydrates into monosaccharides – glucose, fructose, and galactose.

Nut: a dry fruit from a plant or a tree that is usually contained in a pod, which hardens into a shell as the fruit ages. Examples of nuts include walnuts, pecans, and cashews. A peanut is not actually a nut, but a legume. Nuts contain fiber, healthy fats, protein, and vitamin E.

Nutritionist: someone who has an interest in nutrition, and / or who has studied nutrition. A nutritionist may not have the same education as a dietitian, or may not have the same formal training in a hospital or community setting.

Pesticides: a chemical mixture that is used to get rid of "pests" that can cause damage to plants. Pesticides are used in many places, from massive farms to tiny gardens to keep insects, rodents, and harmful organisms away from plants. The governments in different countries keep watch on the use of pesticides in the foods that we eat, because high amounts of pesticides can be harmful to your health and to the general health of the environment.

Phytonutrients: substances found in plant-based foods that area really beneficial to your body. Similar to antioxidants, scientists have found that they help make your immune system stronger. Flavenoids in chocolate and lycopene in tomatoes are phytonutrients.

Polysaccharides: long chains of carbohydrates. They are also called complex carbohydrates. Mostly, when you eat them, they are broken down into monosaccharides and used for energy by your body. However, fiber, which is a kind of polysaccharide, can't be digested by the body.

Preservatives: chemicals that are added to foods to keep them from spoiling. Some preservatives, like nitrites, which are used to preserve meats like bacon and hot dogs, may be harmful to your body if you eat them in large quantities over a long period of time.

Pulses: the edible seeds of legumes, like beans and peas.

Rice milk: a beverage like milk that is made from brown rice. It is a great option for vegetarians and those with a lactose intolerance. Be sure that when you get rice milk that it is enriched with protein, vitamin D, and calcium.

Ripe: when a plant-based food is finished growing and is ready to eat. There are enzymes in food that break down carbohydrates into simple sugars, which help them to ripen and taste sweeter.

Saturated fat : a kind of fat that is solid at room temperature that is usually found in animal-based food. These foods include butter, beef, and chicken skin. Palm and coconut oils are plant-based foods that also contain saturated fats. Eating too many foods that are high in saturated fats can cause blood cholesterol levels to be high, which can be bad for the heart.

Seeds: the part of a plant that comes from the fruit, which can be placed in the ground to grow a new plant. Not all seeds are edible, but many are, including pumpkin, sunflower, and sesame seeds. Seeds are a rich source of fiber, healthy fats, and protein.

Simple sugar: the simplest sugar units, like the monosaccharides glucose, fructose, and galactose, and the disaccharides lactose, and sucrose.

Soy (also known as soya): a plant that produces a legume that is very high in protein and iron. Soy beans are used to make many products, including tofu and soy milk, and are a healthy choice for vegetarians and non-vegetarians alike.

Soy milk: the liquid made when soy beans are crushed in water and drained. Some people choose to drink soy milk because they are vegetarian or because they have a lactose intolerance. Soy milks are often fortified to include the same vitamins and minerals as cow's milk. Major producers of soy milk fortify their milks so that they are equal, in terms of micronutrient values, to cow's milk. However, they may contain less calcium.

Steel-cut oats: less processed than regular oats, they have a high nutritional value and can be used for oatmeal in the morning. Steel cut oats have a nutty flavor and crunchy texture. They take longer to cook than regular oats, so if time is short in the morning, plan to make them the night before and reheat them for breakfast the next day.

Stress: the body's reaction to a certain situation, and often a change, which makes you feel nervous, anxious, or frustrated. This reaction can have an affect on your appetite and on how much you will eat. For some, it may mean that they eat more than usual to cope with the stress, while for others, it can have the opposite effect, causing them to eat less than normal. It has been shown that exercise can help people manage stress.

Tofu: a food with a very mild, nutty taste that is made from soy milk. It is a rich source of protein and iron. It is typically sold in blocks and comes in a variety of forms: extra-firm and firm tofu can be used in stir-fries or added to salads, or grain dishes, while soft tofu can be used in soups, smoothies, and desserts.

Trans fats: unsaturated fat that is chemically changed and added to foods to give them a longer "shelf life." They can be found in processed foods, such as pastries, crackers, and snack foods. However, because scientists have discovered that trans fats are not healthy, more and more manufacturers are no longer using trans fats in their foods. You can see how much trans fat is in your food by reading the nutritional label.

Umami: a fifth taste – a savory or "meaty" taste – that has been discovered, in addition to the tastes of sour, sweet, bitter, and salty.

Unsaturated fat: fat that comes from a plant and sometimes an animal source, like a fish, that is a liquid at room temperature. Eating unsaturated fats can help keep good fats at the right level in blood and can keep bad fats lower.

Vegetarian: someone who chooses not to eat food that comes from an animal, choosing instead to eat foods that are plant based, like breads and cereals, fruits, vegetables and legumes, nuts, and seeds.

Wheat germ: the seed part within a grain of wheat. It is the best-known source of vitamin E and is a great source of protein, riboflavin (a B vitamin), calcium, and zinc. It is a nice, nutty addition to many different foods, including pancakes, hot cereals, baked goods, and even pasta dishes.

Whole grain: a grain that has all of its parts intact. These parts are the bran (the outer layer that provides fiber and some B vitamins), the endosperm (the middle part that provides carbohydrates and protein), and the germ, (the part inside the endosperm that contains B vitamins, vitamin E and other antioxidants). Whole grain foods contain more nutrients than foods made with processed grains, which have had different parts of the grain removed.

Yum: a word to describe something delicious!